What ⌐

Andrew Patterson
Stu has an uncanny complex material in a w ...., promotes understanding and learning, but also highlights the practical significance and application of the topic.

His knowledge is based on an in-depth understanding of relevant research and also, perhaps more importantly, practical and professional experience. There is a distinct dearth of experts in deception (and its detection) in New Zealand and it appears as if Stu is leading the field.

Brian Henderson
Always insightful, always interesting, always entertaining and that's the Truth.

Connor Parry
Oh definitely, the stuff you put up is very informative, and it is why I have such an interest for the science. I particularly enjoy the 'what's this person's expression' where you take a picture of someone's face, say a celebrity, and ask what we think the expression is. I also found that analysis you did of that American presidential debate very informative. The way you described what you saw, it made perfect sense as I was reading what you had written and watching the debate for myself.

Dave Storr
Stu is a thought-provoking innovator who challenges his supporters to analyse photographs, comments and video clips. He then always makes the time to acknowledge all his followers views by offering his expert guidance.

Jeana Wadsworth
You gave me some true insight regarding a family situation that was extremely sensitive to me to be able to make a move forward to repair some heartfelt damage. I took your advice, considered and weighed the options and took action. Today, I have a relationship again with my family that I cannot acknowledge without your help. You have great insight on people. I appreciate it so much!

Debra Schwinn

I am a mental health professional, and am currently working towards licensure as a mental health counselor specialising in trauma and crisis that is directed toward children. Clients in the counseling arena are there due to their experiences or their own actions. In most aspects of counseling, the counselor needs to have a firm grasp on understanding body language, and the most effective counselors will be able to pick up on the smallest of clues towards how the client is truly feeling. What Stu offers through his research, innate desire to teach the general public, and his mentoring to professionals like me about body language is exceptional. I have gained insurmountable confidence in knowing I have the ability to understand those I work with better than they may even know themselves, just through staying in tune to their body language in different situations. Because Stu has made such an enormous impact in my life, I have full confidence that any individual, in any profession, will find his information indispensable. Stu will also become one of your most valuable professional contacts. I urge you to read his book.

Luca Turina

I've read quite a lot of books on the subject already but SDL's programs do what all books fail to do, it shows how to "use" your knowledge of non-verbal communication in every day life while all the books I've read just tell you about non-verbal communication and what different things mean. Your program actually does that while at the same time making people a lot more aware of body language in every day life. Already I pick up a lot more because subconsciously, I'm now always switched on and looking for non-verbal / behavioural clues whereas before the program – even though I knew a lot already – I hardly picked up anything because I wasn't really looking. I was – just as Sherlock Holmes said – seeing but not observing.

Michael Reis

Stu's programs for me are a dream come true! As someone who was known to be able to spot things before, it has only increased my ability and my understanding of what I'm seeing. As a self-defence instructor and tactical trainer and working security for the last 11 years I know the need for these courses! If you can spot "off" behaviour or even just know your own triggers and emotions as they emerge you are doing yourself a huge favour! I'm very pleased and honoured to be a part of Stu Dunn's programs and with his background and use of resources you can't go wrong! Thank you for providing these courses!

TRUE LIES

A Guide to Reading Faces, Interpreting Body Language and Detecting Deception in the Real World

STU DUNN

First Published September 2013
By: Stu Dunn
           Raumati Beach
           Wellington
           New Zealand
Website: www.MicroExpressions.co.nz
Blog: www.StuDunn.com
Twitter: @StuDunn1
Facebook: /sdlmicroexpressions

Cover Photographs: Dean Baines
Special thanks to Harcourts Paraparaumu and Peter Venner Motors
for locations, and Harcourts Paraparaumu, Bridget Dunn, Callan
Dunn Dodson & Caitlin McCleave for helping bring the cover to life in
person.

ISBN-13: 978-1481940177
ISNB-10: 1481940171

Disclaimer. This book references true personal stories, books,
textbooks, studies, websites and other resources – all care has been
taken to ensure appropriate acknowledgement or referencing. All
images within this book are owned or considered public domain after
research.

Stu Dunn, Founder of SDL Behavioural Science Consultancy and Head Consultant, International Speaker, FACS Certified, Micro Expressions, Body Language & Deception Detection Expert.

 Stu Dunn is the first Facial Action Coding System (FACS) Certified consultant in New Zealand. Stu has had a natural interest in human behaviour and non-verbal communication for most of his life. Stu's continued study of psychology, body language, micro expressions and FACS has helped him become New Zealand's leading expert in micro expressions, emotional surveillance and FACS (FACS is the most detailed de-coding of the face, and universally recognized by psychologists and physiologists worldwide).

Stu is also one of the first in the world to achieve Master Level on Humintell's Mix Elite Micro Expressions software. Stu has been studying body language since 2001, and has worked with participants from New Zealand, Australia, United States, United Kingdom, India, Canada, Germany, Afghanistan, Portugal, Switzerland and Sri Lanka so far. This includes working with participants from the NZ Defence, IRD Fraud Investigators, Sri Lankan Customs, Homeland Security, Telecom NZ and Vodafone to name a few. Stu is also part of the Human Behaviour Academy.

Stu's areas of expertise include: micro expressions, emotions and emotional surveillance, body language, deception, interviewing, training, business consulting, video analysis (evaluating truthfulness & credibility), FACS coding (videos, pictures and animation), sales training, assistance with criminal and private investigations.

Outside of behavioural science, Stu practices martial arts. In 1999 he began Wing Chun Kung Fu, and has been teaching the Qian Li Dao Academy style of Wing Chun since 2005. Stu has also been trained in massage, has a Certificate in Hypnotherapy (January 2010) and has written a fantasy book (Sarophia, 2004). Stu and his wife Bridget are successful in the real estate industry, and enjoy the flexibility this allows for their family.

"Education is the most powerful weapon which you can use to change the world." - Nelson Mandela

Dedication

This book is dedicated to my family, whom I love dearly. You have taught me that the most important sending and receiving is in the home.

Acknowledgements

My first thank you is an easy one – my beautiful Bridget. I can honestly say that it is because of you that this book exists, and that I developed any of the SDL programs. You encourage me, challenge me, you became FACS Certified in support, and you've stayed up all hours helping me with consulting work. You have ensured I've had the time to write and you're always a sounding board for my ideas. Most of all though, you've put up with living with a behavioural scientist who sometimes sees far too much. Thank you my love.

Next I would like to thank Vicktorya Stone and Ben Maher, top SDL consultants and personal friends. Vic – you really stepped up and dedicated a lot of your time to editing and feedback, for which I'm extremely grateful. Ben – having known you since you begun Wing Chun Kung Fu at the end of 2005, I think you've found your niche in the behavioural sciences. Thank you for all your support, editing and feedback, as well as support with the 101 and 202 Certification Workshops. Thank you both.

Huge thank you for the testimonials at the front of the book, and to all the contributors for Chapter 18; Adrian Solis, Anne-mari van Staden, Ben Maher, Blanca Cobb, Bridget Dunn, Craig 'CJB' Baxter, Eric Goulard, Eyes for Lies (aka Renee), Michael Lynes, Robert Phipps, Sachchidanand Swami, Suzanne Masefield, and Vicktorya Stone.

Thank you to my mentors, as without you I wouldn't have the knowledge or tools to know where to begin. In particular, thank you to Erika Rosenberg and Maggie Pazian for your FACS teachings. Also a special thanks to all the authors who have acted as my mentors with your writing – thank you for putting in the countless hours to build the amazing library of research that I sourced to put this book together.

Thanks to my mother Rose, who has a great eye for editing.

Lastly, a huge thank you to all you special people who have liked, commented, shared and promoted and supported me through Facebook (www.facebook.com/sdlmicorexpresions) and Twitter (@StuDunn1) – you're awesome!

CONTENTS

"A lie gets halfway around the world before the truth has a chance to get its pants on."
- Winston Churchill

PART 3: DETECTING DECEPTION – THE SCIENCE OF EVALUATING TRUTHFULNESS AND CREDIBILITY

PART 4: THE APPLICATION OF THE SCIENCE

"Men do not understand books until they have a certain amount of life, or at any rate no man understands a deep book, until he has seen and lived at least part of its contents."
-   Ezra Pound

Foreword

"The beginning is in the end."

Foreword written by Eric Goulard, Non-Verbal & Body Language Expert.

After a long evolution among mammals, man has found its way to become the ultimate predator. Modern man – homo sapiens – have only had a short time of existence in comparison, his brain the result of this evolution. His primitive brain allows him to act and react unconsciously and ultra-fast. Thus, the limbic part of the brain controls the reflexes and allows everyone to survive in a world full of danger. Emotions are the result of this cerebral layer that never stops working, just like anti-virus software working in the background on your computer. Man or woman, young or old, man or primate in the jungle, we can not *not* feel emotions. These emotions are ubiquitous; they govern our lives and guide us in our choices. We do not choose to feel one emotion or another. We are always experiencing, and they change with our interactions with others.

Our emotions can change very quickly depending on what we perceive. A positive emotion can mutate quickly to become a negative emotion and back to positive thereafter. A simple smell of pizza or hot chocolate can arouse positive emotions in us, or smelling something rotten can call forth disgust. It's the same thing for perfumes and scents but more subtle and barely noticeable. For example, in relationships, we are able to identify quite unconsciously odours by our partner when they feel excitement. A simple touch on the arm or a glance can create an emotion that has a physiological consequence. Their body reacts, noses and brains perceive unconsciously.

As we interact with others, communication is complex. We need to manage interactions, consider our actions and anticipate their reactions. In situations of tension or stress, you will see many changes occur in the behaviour of your audience that will tell you they feel a discomfort. In a negotiation or during any meeting (including a romantic meeting), you will have a significant head start on your partner if you are able to identify the occurrence of these losses of comfort and if you can get it in touch with the verbal.

Stu Dunn has done a great job by concentrating techniques and modern methods that allow everyone to better understand how humans work. You will learn to recognize facial expressions, and emotions. Cognitive science has experienced strong growth in recent years. The first to have mentioned universality of emotions was Charles Darwin in 1872 in his book "*The Expression of the Emotions in Man and Animals.*" In 1966, two psychologists, Haggard and Isaacs, discovered micro expressions quite by chance. They analysed the films made during psychotherapy sessions. In 1972, Paul Ekman has demonstrated the universality of primary emotions. And since then, studies have continued to flow, mainly in the United States. Today, more than 75 studies demonstrate the universality of emotions. Micro expressions clearly indicate what emotions a person feels, at the precise moment the micro expression appears. It is a reliable indicator of emotion.

In this book, Stu Dunn also speaks at length about the gestures that betray us all. Don't forget that expressions and micro-movements are expressed throughout the body. When we communicate with other people, we want to express things, and our gestures accentuate words. In other cases, we may want to hide things from others. While communicating, one part is what we wish to communicate, however what we wish to hide can still show unintentionally.

Our entire body communicates, often without us realising it. Slip behaviour, contradictory gestures, body leakage, illustrations, handling, etc. we are able to produce multiple actions and behaviours that betray us. These are indicators of the state of person with whom you are communicating.

In the third part, you will learn to recognise the signals specific to the lie detection. So let there be no mistake, you will see no Pinocchio nose! It would be too easy. There is no reliable signal telling us a person is lying. Interactions with the environment and signals indicating stress, including gestures consolation, indicate that something is happening. You will have to determine what.

The subject is fascinating because it goes deep into human nature. Lying has always existed and is not about to disappear... I do not just mean politicians, negotiation meetings or a poker game. I also talk about life at home, in your couple or with your family and friends!

Finally, through the stories of professionals, you will learn how the science is used today in practice on the ground. You will know the techniques, tips and tricks to better understand others and improve your relationships.

This book could quickly become your reference on the subject of non-verbal communication, one that you will take with you, always accessible and available! One thing is certain, after reading this book you will not look at people the same way again!

CHAPTER 1
Introduction to True Lies and the Science of Non-Verbal Behaviour

"Any emotion, if it is sincere, is involuntary" - Mark Twain

Introduction

A man stands between you and your car; arms folded, legs apart, with narrowed eyes glaring at you with tightened lips. Are you in danger? A woman smiles at you from across the bar and moves her drink to one side. Was that an invitation? Your teenager comes home late and explains with hands in pockets and a single shoulder shrug how someone else damaged the car. Are you being lied to? You have worked hard on this deal, with the paperwork about to be signed. You notice the man you have been negotiating with is reading the contract with a half smile, and as he sees you watching, replaces his smile with a more serious look. Has this man been deceptive in order to gain a better price? You ask the seller of the car if there is anything wrong with it, and they respond with a stutter, pause, then a vague "Not that I recall" answer. All of these situations come from someone's real life experiences. Everyday we have questions, such as: Does he / she like me? What are they thinking? Are they in a good mood? Do they like the idea? Did he just lie? Am I buying a lemon? Should I do business with this person? Do I trust him with my kids? Are they the best person for the job? Can I see myself with this person for the rest of my life?

Everyday we have so many questions, and for these to remain unanswered can sometimes be accompanied with an ever increasing list of insecurities. In my opinion people and relationships are one of the greatest mysteries in life, and as I have a deep drive to better understand people I was drawn to the behavioural sciences. And it is through my learning and witnessing so many who could benefit from learning that I found my passion in helping people to understand non-verbal communication – and to avoid deception.

To open this book is to take a step towards improving your understanding of people, and with this understanding comes the opportunity to improve relationships with family members, co-workers, friends – or even to find that special someone.

Why I Wrote This Book

I wrote *True Lies: A Guide to Reading Faces, Interpreting Body Language and Detecting Deception in the Real World* for a number of reasons – some of which I have already mentioned.

There are already a lot of books (and other resources) out there on the subjects of facial expressions, body language and detecting deception, with some being very good in my opinion, some overly detailed (aimed at the scientific community and less digestible by the non-scientific community), and some quite under detailed (and horribly inaccurate). This is where I saw a gap: for a guide that combines research on the face, body language and detecting deception through behavioural cues into one simple-to-read "handbook". This book is not intended to be a textbook, nor does it cover *all* research and authors in these areas. I made the decision early on that this book must be;

1)   Simple to read,
2)   Attract both experts in the field as well as welcoming fresh interest,
3)   Promote the science and shed light on myths and incorrect assumptions, and
4)   To encourage better communication and understanding in all areas of people's lives.

This last point is (as depicted on the front cover and introduced above) the purpose of this book: to get the message out to the world that becoming proficient with reading emotions, micro expressions and body language are useful in all areas of life; such as relationships, the corporate world, at home with the family and as consumers. The more people that become proficient with detecting deception can help to create an honest environment. Why bother lying if everyone will call you on it?

"One of the greatest rewards of becoming proficient with detecting deception is that once you eliminate your environment of dishonesty, you're free to invest your efforts elsewhere. Maintaining an environment of intelligent trust takes up much less energy than constantly watching over your shoulder." - Stu Dunn

Detecting Deception at Home

Having Bridget and I both being proficient with detecting deception (and also both FACS certified) keeps our kids honest! We have 3 kids living at home: Callan, Alex and Caitlin. The kids are *much* more likely to be honest straight away (what everyone encourages of course, however often the natural tendency would be to either flat out deny or blame someone else). If a lie does come out, it doesn't tend to last long before being uncovered.

It has taken me a long time to be able to switch off seeing "everything" at home, with a general rule at home that Bridget & I try not to analyse each other. I'm not talking about deception, rather the micro expressions, body language and voice cues that alert me that there is a variance from the normal baseline. I find that for the most part I can switch off, however sometimes I find it really challenging to notice a subtle mood change with Bridget and not say anything.

Overall, I want to explain behavioural science – the interactions and communications with and between people – in such a way that this information is accessible to everyone, and from this provide readers with practical ways to learn *and* apply this information straight away with the purpose of improving their own lives in so many various ways.

Who Is This Book Written For?

This book has such a wide audience as it is written for anyone who interacts with another human being. It is written for the salesperson who wants to improve the presentation, observe when to ask for the sale, come across more professionally and ultimately increase their sales. It is written for the consumer who takes their car to the garage to get a quote, who is looking to buy their first home, and for those who want to know if that is the best price they can get. It is written for the business owner and manager who look after staff, for the recruiter and interviewer who must stay alert for false statements, for the negotiator, and the loan officer discussing applications. This book is written for the couple who want to improve their communication, the woman wanting to make a good impression on her first date, the mother wanting to understand her children and the son wanting to make sure his parents are happy.

This book is written for you – as at some stage in your life – you will have to interact with people.

My Special Message

There are certain organisations that I feel would benefit from this book, such as anywhere salespeople's faces are displayed, as fake teeth-clenched smiles are not welcoming to customers. All areas in the security environment would profit, along with the financial industry and Government departments.

However the specific organisation I feel this book would do the most good is the police force. In my opinion, many a police force is still run by old-school rules (New Zealand in particular), where the PEACE model of interviewing is all that they require, and refuse to look at ways to further improve (not replace) on what they currently do. My message is; Stay open minded, take what works and add it to what you do.

"It is much simpler to buy books than to read them and easier to read them than to absorb their contents." - William Osler

How To Get The Most From This Book

I have divided the book into four parts, with the first three parts having suggested exercises to complete at the end. The suggested answers can be found in the appendix.

To know and not to do is not yet to know.

I think it was Lao Tzu who said the above quote, and I often reiterate this by asking; "After reading a book on riding a bike, can you ride a bike?" The answer is no, as you have only *read* about riding a bike. To learn how to *actually* ride a bike, you must practice riding on a real bike. The same applies to this book. To know and not to do is not yet to know. This is why I included exercises – so you can *do* to help you *know*.

Other Recommendations

If you have any questions, would like to continue your education, wish to organise a live workshop etc – these are the best ways to stay in touch and receive updates:

Website: www.MicroExpressions.co.nz
Blog: www.StuDunn.com
Twitter: @StuDunn1
Facebook: /sdlmicroexpressions

Personal Stories

Throughout the book I have included gray boxes that include my personal opinions, stories, and other information that I hope will both interest and help readers grasp the information in a more informal manner. When I run my live workshops I am relaxed, chatty and approachable – and these gray boxes are my attempt to bring some of this style to these pages.

The Science of Non-Verbal Behaviour

For some of you this book will be an introduction to the science of non-verbal behaviour, therefore I will introduce how I will tackle this book. Non-verbal behaviour or communication has been referred to as body language for a long time; however researchers have defined non-verbal communication to include virtually all communication – with the exclusion of the spoken word (Knapp, 1972). This implies that there is more to non-verbal communication than just body language, and can include how someone dresses or how they arrange their office (Henley, 1977). Overall, if you are not paying enough attention to non-verbal communication you could be missing a lot of the message that is really being sent.

The Five Channels of Communication

The key channels of communication that I cover in this book are: the face, gestures and body language, the voice, verbal styles and verbal statements. Chapters 2–9 discuss the face along with supporting research, Chapters 10–12 cover gestures and body language and Chapter 13 introduces the voice, verbal style and verbal statements.

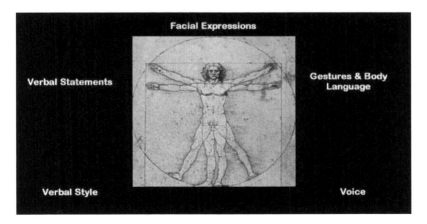

DID YOU KNOW?

* 55% of the messages that we convey to other people are transmitted through body language, 38% is in the tone of voice, and only 7% in the words we use (*when verbal context is ambiguous).

* According to studies, 65-95% of most messages are communicated nonverbally.

* Several studies have shown that 90% of the decisions we make are based on emotion - we then use logic to justify our actions.

* Research has shown that a normal everyday person will lie on average 3 times for every 10 minutes of conversation.

* Research shows that people that have not been trained to detect micro expressions and other clues only has around a 54% chance of catching lies – which isn't much better than chance.

* The combination of fraud, theft, identity & employee theft, embezzlement, information leaks, false qualifications & experience, falsifying credit and other information on documents, accounts for tens of billions of dollars lost each year.

* How much could it cost you *not* to do something? Through training people can easily become 80%+ accurate at detecting hidden emotions (micro expressions), as well as learning to more accurately interpret body language and spot deceptive behaviour – including written statements.

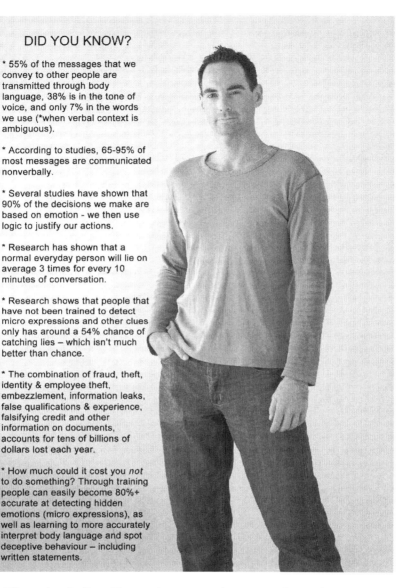

"Everybody lies. Every day, every hour, awake, asleep, in his dreams, in his joy, in his mourning." - Mark Twain

PART 1

FACIAL EXPRESSIONS

CHAPTER 2
Introduction to Facial Expressions

"Being able to read others' emotions can give you insights, not only to their emotional states but their intentions, motivations, personalities, trustworthiness and credibility. Emotions can inform us of malicious intent, hidden information, or downright deception" - David Matsumoto

Introduction

Of all the channels of non-verbal communication, the face is the most complex of signalling systems, the most studied channel by scientists, and reflects both voluntary and involuntary reactions and emotional states (Matsumoto & Hwang, 2012). The face is an amazing source of information about human behaviour, as it displays emotion, pain, and divulges brain function and pathology (Ekman, 1993; Russell, 1994; Craig, Hyde & Patrick, 1991; Ekman, Davidson & Friesen, 1990; Fox & Davidson, 1988; Katsikitis & Pilowsky, 1988; Rinn, 1984). Learning the skills to read another's emotions can provide valuable insights into an individual's intentions, motivations and credibility (Matsumoto & Hwang, 2012).

The face tells us the shape, skin colour, bone structure, size and general location of features, referred to as static facial signals. Static signals as the name suggests remain the same. They indicate permanent aspects of the face, such as an individuals' ethnic background (although in extreme cases this too can be altered through plastic surgery for example). The second category of facial signals is slow facial signals. These accumulate on the face over time, which includes the gradual increasing of wrinkles and skin tone etc. The final category is the rapid facial signals which include facial muscle movements such as emotions, micro expressions, and facial emblems such as raising the eyebrows in questioning (Ekman & Friesen, 2003).

"A little more than one hundred years ago, Charles Darwin wrote that facial expressions of emotion are universal, not learned differently in each culture; that they are biologically determined, the product of man's evolution. Since Darwin's time many writers have emphatically disagreed. Just recently, however, scientific investigations have conclusively settled this question, showing that the facial appearance of at least some emotions…is indeed universal, although there are cultural differences in when these expressions are shown" (Ekman & Friesen, 2003, p.23).

Why study micro expressions and the face?

Micro expressions occur when someone wants to hide a felt emotion – so it will always depend on the person (whether they care about hiding the emotion or not) and the situation (whether it would be bad for the person to be caught expressing that emotion, such as a child trying not to smile at a funeral) as to whether someone will leak an expression.

Micro expressions were first discovered by Haggard and Isaacs over 40 years ago. They published a report on these expressions in 1966, which they called "micromomentary" expressions. The article they wrote was entitled *Micro-momentary facial expressions as indicators of ego mechanisms in psychotherapy*. Many subsequent studies have been conducted based on the research by Haggard and Isaacs, but the discovery of micro expressions should be attributed to them.

Emotions are immediate, automatic, and unconscious reactions – and are perhaps the closest thing humans have to a universal language. Truly felt emotions and expressions occur involuntarily, without thought or intention, where false expressions have to be displayed intentionally. The face is a dual system, showing both intentional and involuntary emotions – and sometimes a blended expression of genuine and fake displays. Put simply, the face displays what the person wants to show, and what the person wants to conceal.

Expressions are likely to be false when they are asymmetrical, the duration of expression is either too long or too short, or the timing of the expression in relation to the speech is not synchronized. The face can also be a valuable source of information for detecting deceit, because the face can lie and tell the truth – and often does both at the same time (Ekman, 2009).

The Seven Universal Expressions

Charles Darwin was one of the first people known for researching emotion, believing emotions to be biological and universal. Paul Ekman and Wallace V. Friesen studied universal emotions in Papua New Guinea, verifying that even cultures which have no contact with the outside world share these seven universal emotions: happiness, surprise, contempt, sadness, fear, disgust and anger. Therefore, the seven universal expressions are expressed by everyone, regardless of race, culture, age or gender. Studies done by David

Matsumoto demonstrated that sighted and blind individuals produce the same facial muscle movements in response to emotional stimuli - even when they are blind from birth. This indicates that emotions are innate; we are born with the knowledge of how to express these emotions through facial expressions.

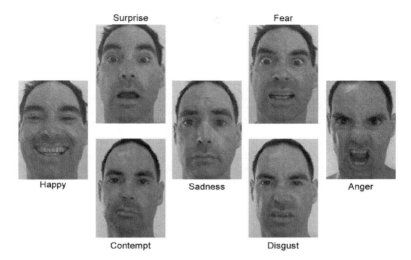

Cultural differences in non-verbal communication do start appearing when it comes to gestures, in particular, hand and facial emblems. Even areas within cities can have their own gesturing language and meaning. I'll explore a few of these in Part 2.

Tip: In practicing online micro expressions training, I recommend watching the nose and using your peripheral vision to take in any changes with the eyes, forehead and lower face.

Robert Plutchik's Wheel of Emotions

I have been asked a number of times about *where* certain emotions would fit within the seven universal emotions. An exercise I ran during a couple of my workshops seemed to really help participants appreciate how this all fits together.

First I would ask; "What are some emotions you can think of? – I would then write them on a whiteboard. Of course, the first ones called were the seven universal emotions; happiness, sadness, surprise, fear, anger, disgust and contempt. But then other emotions were called out, such as excitement, depression, shock, terror, rage, repulsed and scorn. In this example, excitement would fit into the "happiness" category, along with joy, amused etc. There's a happiness scale, from mild right through to very strong. Anger has a large range; between irritated or annoyed through to rage. Anything in between would fit into the anger category. This is why I find Robert Plutchik's Wheel of Emotions helpful – as the seven emotions *nearly* fit perfectly into his model – I think it is a great illustration of these ranges within each category of emotion.

We also have to be aware of what is not classed as an emotion; does the emotion last quite a long time? It could be a **mood**. Is this how the person usually acts or feels? It could be a **personality trait**. Lastly, is the person is severely breaching our social norms for emotional behaviour? It could be a psychopathological disorder. For example, someone could express fear (a relatively temporary emotion), they could be naturally apprehensive (experiencing a mood that lasts longer than the emotion), they could be a shy person (a personality trait), or they could have panic attacks, phobias / extreme anxiety (a psychopathological disorder) (Matsumoto, 2012).

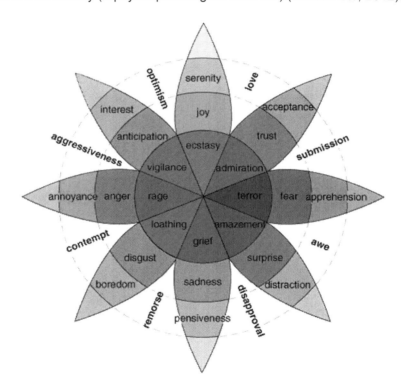

Macro, Micro and Subtle Expressions

There are three types of facial expressions of emotions known as macro expressions, micro expressions and subtle expressions.

1) *Macro expressions* typically last from 1/2 second to 4 seconds: we see them in our daily interactions with people all of the time.

2) *Micro expressions* last less than 1/2 second, sometimes as fast as 1/25 of a second. Micro expressions are signs of concealed emotions that leak out when people are in *high stake situations* but are trying to control their feelings. By high stake I mean situations where it is important whether the person shows an emotion. For example, someone being interviewed for a job; the applicant is motivated to come across well in order to obtain the job, so if they're feeling a negative emotion such as contempt or disgust during the interview, they're likely to try to hide it – which leaks out in the form of a micro expression.

In regards to everyday living, micro expressions are absolutely essential in understanding how people around you really feel. Research shows that emotional intelligence impacts on how successful people are in their careers, and being able to read emotional signals is an extremely important part of this emotional intelligence.

3) *Subtle expressions* occur when a person is just starting to feel an emotion or when their emotional response to a situation is relatively low or they are able to disguise their expression well. Recently published research showed a high correlation between recognising subtle expressions and being able to detect deceit.

What is FACS?

The Facial Action Coding System (FACS) is a tool for evaluating and understanding facial expressions and emotion and has provided the scientific community with a systematic way of coding muscle movements in the face and classifying specific muscle combinations into emotional categories. Developed by Dr. Paul Ekman, FACS is still the most widely used tool for classifying facial behaviour and interpreting people's emotional states.

Terms of the Face

In order to describe changes in facial appearance you should become familiar with several terms which refer to particular areas and features of the face and the changes in them.

Glabella	Area above the root of the nose between the eyebrows.
Root of Nose	The beginning of the nose between the eyes.
Eye Cover Fold	The skin between the eyebrows and the upper eyelid.
Lower Eyelid Furrow	Below the lower eyelid.
Infraorbital Furrow	The area running from near the inner corner of the eye and following the cheek bone.
Nostril Wings	The fleshy skin of the side of each nostril.
Nasolabial Furrow	The area adjacent to the nostril wings that run down and outwards beyond the lip corners. In some people it is permanently etched in the face; if so, it will deepen with certain movements.
Philtrum	The vertical depression in the centre of the upper lip directly under the tip of the nose.
Chin Boss	The skin covering the bone of the chin.
Sclera	The white part of the eyeball.

Terms of the Face Image

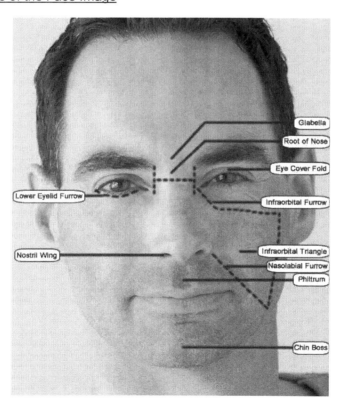

How to Read the FACS Action Unit Images

Action Units (AUs) represent the muscular activity that produces the changes in facial appearance. Each AU is identified by a number and name, for example, AU4 Brow Lowerer. The location of the "boxed" number in the FACS Action Unit Images shows approximately where the muscle **emerges** (or the origin) from the bony structure. The other end of the line indicates approximately where the muscle **attaches** to the soft tissue of the face. When the muscle contracts it pulls toward where the muscle **emerges** (Ekman, Friesen, & Hager, 2002).

Upper Face Action Units

The images of the upper face action units (AUs) shows the muscles responsible for changing the appearance of the eyebrows, forehead, eye cover fold, and the upper and lower eyelids. AU5 (Upper Lid Raiser) is excluded as it is hidden in the eye socket. AU43 (Eye Closure) AU45 (Blink) and AU46 (Wink) are also excluded (Ekman, Friesen, & Hager, 2002).

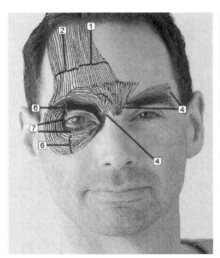 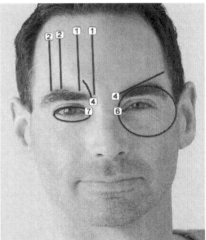

Lower Face Up / Down Action Units

The five major groups of lower face action units are *Up/Downs*, *Horizontals*, *Obliques*, *Orbitals*, and the fifth group involves a number of *Miscellaneous* actions (Ekman, Friesen, & Hager, 2002).

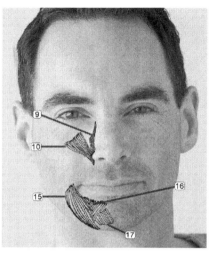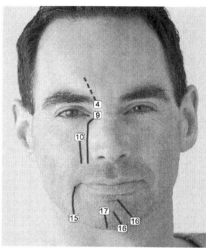

Lower Face Horizontal Action Units

The Lip Stretcher (AU20) pulls the lip corners laterally, and the Dimpler (AU14) tightens the lip corners and pulls them inwards (Ekman, Friesen, & Hager, 2002).

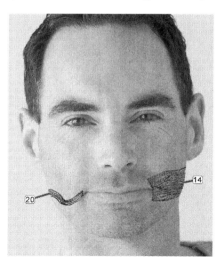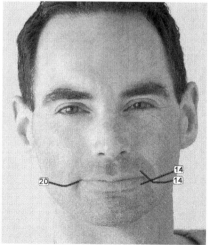

Lower Face Oblique Action Units

These are called *Oblique* due to the action of each involves pulling the skin of the face upward at an oblique angle (Ekman, Friesen, & Hager, 2002).

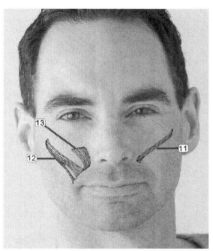 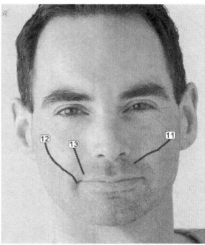

Lower Face Orbital Action Units

These are the primary muscles that underlie lower face *Orbital* actions (Ekman, Friesen, & Hager, 2002).

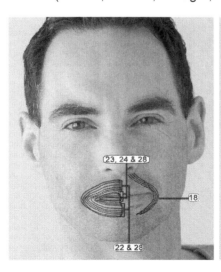 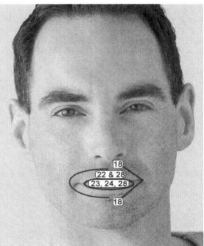

FACS Action Unit Intensity Scoring

When evidence of any specific AU is absent, the face is in a neutral (or baseline) scoring condition. When evidence of an AU is present, intensity of an Action Unit can be scored on a five-point ordinal scale. The letters A, B, C, D, and E refer to the intensity of an action (Ekman, Friesen, & Hager, 2002).

Relation between the Scale of Evidence and Intensity Scores

Trace	Slight	Marked	Pronounced	Severe	Extreme	Maximum
A	B		C		D	E

A level refers to a *trace* of the action; B, *slight* evidence; C, *marked* or *pronounced*; D, *severe* or *extreme*; and E, *maximum* evidence.

E.g. 4A would indicate the faint trace of a frown, whereas 4E would have the brows lowered as much as possible – maximum intensity.

For your reference, the following page lists the most common FACS Codes.

Important Note: The several pages included in this book on FACS coding are in no way a substitute for proper FACS training, and are only included as an introduction to the Facial Action Coding System. The only way to purchase the full FACS training is through Joe Hager's website (http://face-and-emotion.com/dataface/facs/new_version.jsp). Training can be done through self study using the training materials, or through week long training sessions run by the some of the best FACS coders in the world.

Facial Action Coding (FACS) Codes

Upper Face	
AU 1	Inner Brow Raiser
AU 2	Outer Brow Raiser
AU 4	Brow Lowerer
AU 5	Upper Lid Raiser
AU 6	Cheek Raiser
AU 7	Lid Tightener
AU 43	Eye Closure - Optional
AU 45	Blink - Optional
AU 46	Wink - Optional

Lower Face (Up/Down Actions)	
AU 9	Nose Wrinkler
AU 10	Upper Lip Raiser
AU 15	Lip Corner Depressor
AU 16	Lower Lip Depressor
AU 17	Chin Raiser
AU 25	Lips Part
AU 26	Jaw Drop
AU 27	Mouth Stretch

Lower Face (Horizontal Actions)	
AU 14	Dimpler
AU 20	Lip Stretcher

Lower Face (Oblique Actions)	
AU 11	Nasolabial Furrow Deepener
AU 12	Lip Corner Puller
AU 13	Sharp Lip Puller

Lower Face (Orbital Actions)	
AU 18	Lip Pucker
AU 22/22+25	Lip Funneler
AU 23	Lip Tightener
AU 24	Lip Presser
AU 28/26+28	Lips Suck

Head & Eye Positions	
51	Head Turn Left
52	Head Turn Right
53	Head Up
54	Head Down
55	Head Tilt Left
56	Head Tilt Right
57	Head Forward
58	Head Back
61	Eyes Turn Left
62	Eyes Turn Right
63	Eyes Up
64	Eyes Down
65	Walleye
66	Cross-Eye
69	AUs 4, 5 & 7 (alone or in combo) + gazing at someone

Visibility Codes	
70	Brows & forehead not visible
71	Eyes not visible
72	Lower face not visible
73	Entire face not visible
74	Unscorable

Gross Behavior Codes	
40	Sniff
50	Speech
80	Swallow
81	Chewing
82	Shoulder Shrug
84	Head Shake Back & Forth
85	Head Nod Up & Down
91	Flash
92	Partial Flash

Miscellaneous Actions & Supplementary Codes			
AU 8+25	Lips Toward Each Other	AD 33	Blow
AD 19	Tongue Show	AD 34	Puff
AU 21	Neck Tightener	AD 35	Suck
AD 29	Jaw Thrust	AD 36	Bulge
AD 30	Jaw Sideways	AD 37	Lip Wipe
AU 31	Jaw Clencher	AU 38	Nostril Dilator
AD 32	Bite	AU 39	Nostril Compressor

To download a copy of the FACS code sheet, visit
www.microexpressions.co.nz/images/documents/SDL_FACS_Codes.pdf

What is Botox and How It Relates to the Face

Botulinum toxin is a protein and neurotoxin produced by the bacterium called *Clostridium botulinum*. Botulinum toxin can cause botulism, a serious and life-threatening illness in humans and animals. Popularly known by one of its trade names – Botox – it is used for various cosmetic and medical procedures.

Some Side Effects of Botox

A side effect of having Botox procedures on the face for cosmetic purposes is the inability to fully express emotions, with research revealing this can include the inability to fully feel emotions* as well as dulling the ability to detect emotions**. Eric Finzi writes; "William

Shakespeare famously wrote that 'a face is like a book,' and common wisdom has it that our faces reveal our deep-seated emotions. But what if the reverse were also true? What if our facial expressions set our moods instead of revealing them? What if there was actual scientific evidence to support the phrase, 'smile, be happy?'"

Sources: * http://www.livescience.com/8325-botox-limits-ability-feel-emotions.html
** http://www.medicalnewstoday.com/articles/223242.php

Botox and Facial Emblems

Raising the eyebrows can indicate signs of interest, and is often used in normal conversations (along with the eyebrows) as punctuators and to emphasize points. These tend to be absent with individuals who have been Botoxed, which also alters the appearance of emotions (lack of raised eyebrows can alter how fear and surprise appear).

Lowering the brows (also absent with many Botox patients) by themselves can be a subtle sign of anger, however it can also display deep thinking, disapproval, or something as simple as shading the eyes from a bright light or the sun.

"I want my kids to know when I'm pissed, when I'm happy and when I'm confounded. Your face tells a story and it shouldn't be a story about your drive to the doctor's office."
- Julia Roberts

Botox and Parenting

"Botox does likely limit and distort parent-infant communication, possibly making the parent look 'flat' emotionally," says Dr. Ed Tronick, associate professor of paediatrics and psychiatry at the University of Massachusetts. "Facial expressions for parents and young children are really critical ways in which we communicate our intentions or whether we're angry or sad, and that involves this very complex array of all the muscles that go into making facial expressions. So if you limit that range of expression, especially with very young children who are really attuned to reading facial expressions, then you limit the amount of information, the amount of emotion that you communicate using a facial expression."

Source: http://edition.cnn.com/2012/09/20/living/botox-moms

Botox and the False Fear Smile

Dr. G. Jack Brown suggests another interesting side effect on facial expressions and Botox – the "false fear" smile. This is a smile where the upper eyelids will "over-compensate" and raise to make up for the lack of forehead movement, creating what can be described as an alarming smile.

Why Are Eyes Not Covered Here?

A large number of Neuro Linguistic Programming (NLP) practitioners claim that certain eye-movements are reliable indicators of lying. According to this idea, a person looking up to their right suggests a lie whereas looking up to their left is indicative of truth telling. Wiseman, Watt, ten Brinke, Porter, Couper & Rankin (2012) performed three studies to confirm or deny this eye movement which showed no difference with truth tellers or liars (there were however several flaws in their studies). In saying this, in my opinion there is not enough empirical evidence to confirm eye movement as being a reliable indicator of lying or recalling memories (and also excludes any differences related to left and right handed individuals). The most evidence I have found (so far) toward eye movement meanings are from several studies which indicated that looking sideways is associated with accessing memories associated with sound, and slightly less evidence for looking up accessing visual memory. I am pleased that many NLP practitioners who use and teach eye accessing cues *and* baselining rather than having one rule to cover everyone. Overall, I think there is something to eye movement, however due to the lack of empirical evidence, I have not included eye interpretations in this book.

> **Tip:** Pupil dilation (where the blacks of the eyes become larger) is associated with emotional arousal.

Prosopagnosia

As we are discussing the face, it is worth making a special mention to those who can not recognise any face. Prosopagnosia (from the Greek words: "prosopon" meaning face, and "agnosia" meaning not knowing) or face blindness, is extreme difficulty in recognising faces. This is caused usually by some kind of damage to the fusiform gyrus, which is a part of the brain that activates specifically to faces. As people with this condition are unable to utilize the static or slow facial signals for recognition, they tend to use secondary clues such as clothing style, the way they walk, hair colour and style, body shape, and voice. I am personally curious as to whether people suffering from prosopagnosia could still recognise rapid facial signals such as micro expressions as I haven't come across any studies in this area to date.

Emotional Intelligence

Emotional intelligence (EI) can be described as the ability to identify, assess, and control the emotions of oneself and others. Research carried out by the Carnegie Institute of Technology showed that 85% of financial success is due to skills they label under "human engineering," (which includes your personality, ability to communicate, negotiate, and lead), with only 15% of financial success being due to actual technical knowledge. The research also suggested that emotional intelligence alone has an impact on how successful people are in their careers, as reading emotional signals is an important part of building rapport and inter-personal communication. And what is one of the quickest and most effective ways of building emotional intelligence? The answer is to become proficient with reading micro expressions.

Learning How to Read Micro Expressions

There is no way to become proficient with spotting micro expressions without practice, and the most efficient way of initially learning these skills is through online training. Being involved in behavioural science on a daily basis I have been exposed to pretty much all micro expressions online training tools there are on the market. In my professional opinion, there are only three that I would recommend. Check out the demo on each website and discover which one you prefer:

Paul Ekman Group (www.PaulEkman.com)

The Ekman tools for training micro expressions have long exceeded my expectations of value for money, support, usability and of course results in learning to spot micro expressions. The introduction of eMETT 3.0 and eSETT 3.0 are expertly explained by Dr. Paul Ekman himself – and I believe will increase your understanding of micro expressions and subtle expressions in an even shorter period of time than its predecessors. I highly recommend these products as being a small investment to gain lifelong perception.

Humintell (www.Humintell.com)

Dr. David Matsumoto's Humintell has truly specialised in the online training of micro expressions, subtle expressions, identifying deadly intent and the education of different cultures and customs. Humintell is equipped with extremely professional products designed to suit beginners through to master levels.

Centre for Body Language
(www.microexpressionstrainingvideos.com)

The key differences with this online training for me are 1) the situations and 2) the neutral option. Firstly, the situations where you search for micro expressions tend to be in more real life situations (such as having a conversation with a friend). For some people, this may be more difficult to start learning from, whereas for others they seem to have no trouble. Secondly, having the option that no expression (neutral) was shown provides another layer to the training.

My Son Callan Playing Battleships

One afternoon I overheard my son Callan (who was 11) and his step brother Alex (who was 7) playing the old board game; *Battleships*. By the sounds of it, Callan was winning and was using a "secret strategy" that he kept to himself – up until he absolutely knew he was going to win the game.
His strategy?

He would call out the first part of his turn slowly; "My turn, B...." and he'd examine Alex's face. If there was relief, Callan would then say; "No, not B. Hmm, how about C...." If Alex's face gave away that he had a ship on C somewhere, Callan would take his turn. Needless to say, Alex finished the game by trying to hide his face behind a cushion.

There's an application of utilising micro expressions that I hadn't considered!

"The best way to cheer yourself up, is to cheer somebody else up." - Mark Twain

CHAPTER 3
Happiness / Joy

"Trying to be happy by accumulating possessions is like trying to satisfy hunger by taping sandwiches all over your body."
- George Carlin

Introduction

Happiness is a positive emotion and one most of us seek to experience more often, and is used to shape many of our less important daily choices as well as help us with our bigger lifelong choices. Ekman & Friesen (2003) distinguishes happiness into four main states: *pleasure*, *excitement*, *relief*, and lastly *self-concept* (Ekman & Friesen, 2003).

Pleasure involves positive physical sensations, with the opposite being pain. Tony Robbins, a self-help author and motivational speaker, speaks a lot about the push / pull between pain and pleasure. If we want to change a habit (that we no longer wish to have), then all we need do is attach more pain than pleasure to that habit.

Tip: Most people don't know that I was a smoker for around 17 years. Because I really enjoyed it, I associated much more pleasure to continuing to smoke that I did being smoke free. It was only when I started reading a wealth book in the beginning of 2010 that I realised just how much money I was wasting each week on cigarettes, each month, each year. Over the space of a week I slowly switched my associations to smoking from pleasurable to more (financial) pain than pleasure. As soon as the balance tipped and I associated more pain to the habit, I became smoke free.

"The truth is that we can learn to condition our minds, bodies, and emotions to link pain or pleasure to whatever we choose. By changing what we link pain and pleasure to, we will instantly change our behaviours." - Tony Robbins

---

Excitement occurs when something provokes your interest, with the opposite being boredom. You become more present while excited, whereas your attention is difficult to hold while bored. It is also possible to be excited and yet not happy, as it can also blend with fear (in a state of terror) or anger (in a state of rage) and other emotion combinations.

Relief occurs when something that was "not good" stops, such as when pain ceases (pain relief starts to work or an injury heals), hunger (eating creates relief), thirst (drinking), negative emotions (e.g. no longer afraid or sad), and in some cases – happiness-relief is present after a long wait. Happiness in the form of relief can also come from personally completing something that stops the cause of negative emotions.

The form of self-concept happiness occurs when something happens that boosts your self image, such as receiving a compliment, acknowledgement, having an anniversary remembered, basically anything that has you feeling good about yourself.

Tip: Exercise releases endorphins. Endorphins trigger a positive feeling in the body (similar to that of morphine), act as analgesics (which diminishes the perception of pain) and can act as sedatives. They are manufactured in your brain, spinal cord, and many other parts of your body and are released in response to brain chemicals called neurotransmitters. This is how exercise can make you feel happy.

Playing many sports would include all of the happiness states, as would most sexual encounters. Also watching a good comedy could trigger excitement, relief and perhaps even improve ones self esteem. Matsumoto & Hwang sum up Larazus's (1991) triggers for happiness as "goal attainment or accomplishment", and the function of happiness being to motivate future actions (Matsumoto & Hwang, 2012).

Appearance

Genuine smiles – the universal sign of happiness – are expressed with a *Duchenne* smile. This is expressed on the face by the combined contraction of the *zygomaticus major* muscle (which is the voluntary part of a smile and is also engaged when saying "cheese" or clenching a pen in one's teeth), and the *orbicularis oculi* - the cheek raiser (which raises the cheeks and creates or increases crows feet).

The images above show first a neutral face, then progressions of happiness from mild to extreme.

Self-Conditional Happiness

I don't recall how many times I've heard someone say casually; "I'll be happy when I get that job", "I'll be happy when this is all over", "When the kids are grown", "When I finish this work", "When I'm with [someone]", or "When I get some more money". These are such common things to be grateful for, however looking at the language of what people say everyday - are we making our happiness conditional?

Taking a step back, saying "I'll be happy when / if" sends a message - whether true or false - that you're not *currently* happy. If you're not currently happy, then there's the chance that you'll get stuck in the loop to *only* be happy when you reach that job, the perfect relationship, the financial status you desire etc. The loop completes when - not long after gaining what will "make you happy" - another condition is put in place. "Well, now that I have that job, I'll actually be *really* happy once I get that [pay rise, transfer, bonus etc]".

My suggestion is to avoid using the term "I'll be happy when / if". Kids get it – they can be unconditionally happy, and can love unconditionally. Why not try being happy now? For some that is a real stretch, so my thoughts on that are to write down what would have you happy. Sometimes it's as tricky as asking; "What is success?" The answer is different for every individual. Over-achievers get stuck in their own cycle of pushing further and working harder to become successful, without ever defining what is success to them. We are far too often stuck in a world where we are given ideas that aren't our own about certain things, such as the importance of name-brands, super model bodies and constructs of what makes people on TV happy and successful.

So if you're having difficulties being happy right now, take the time to define your idea of happiness. Instead of just saying; "Having enough money, being in a healthy relationship, lots of free time" –

define it. What is enough money? Is it only $200 / week, or is it $1,000? More? Less? Define a healthy relationship, what it means to you - not someone else. How much is "lots" of free time? Is it 1 hour per week or more like 20 hours per week?

Something in particular that I find frustrating are the images of the stereotype rich girl screaming at her parents for not getting her the right coloured car compared to the African kids using squashed plastic bottles as shoes laughing and playing happily with rocks in the dirt...

FACS Codes

Most Common FACS Codes for: Happiness – Action Units (AU's) 6+12	
AU6: Raising of the cheeks	AU12: Raising of the lip corners

Raised Cheeks

| Neutral | Extreme Happiness | Mouth Only Smile |

The raising of the cheeks (the *orbicularis oculi* or FACS Action Unit 6) is the major indicator of genuine happiness, with the first sign being crow's-feet wrinkling around the outer corner of the eyes; the second sign of the cheeks rising is demonstrated in the bunching of skin underneath the eyes. Not everyone shows crow's-feet – often young children and some adults do not show these wrinkles. There are also people who already have quite pronounced deep crow's-feet wrinkles permanently etched around the outer corners of the eyes. Where there are permanent wrinkles in an individual's neutral face, the crow's-feet will deepen and become more obvious when the cheeks are raised.

Tip: Checking for crow's-feet can be one of the most reliable indicators of genuine happiness, and can be detected when someone is trying to mask their happiness behind another emotion. Put even simpler; a natural smile produces wrinkles around the eyes whereas social smiles only engage the mouth.

Pulling Up of the Lip Corners

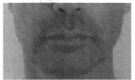  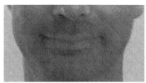

Neutral   Strong Lip Corner Puller   Dimpler Smile

The muscle underlying the *zygomaticus major* (lip corner puller) originates by the cheek bones and attaches at the corner of the lips, pulling in an oblique direction from the lip corners up towards the cheek bone (FACS Action Unit 12).

Optimism versus Delusion

For most of my adult life I've considered myself an optimist. I've certainly been called an optimist - however - I've also been called delusional with my positive attitude and faith in things "turning out how they should". Dictionary.com defines optimism as: "a disposition or tendency to look on the more favourable side of events or conditions and to expect the most favourable outcome". So, at what point does over optimism actually become delusional? When does seeing the world through rose-tinted glasses go too far to the stage of becoming a mental illness? Interesting questions - perhaps ones asked by the pessimist?

"Optimism is the madness of insisting that all is well when we are miserable." - Voltaire

Psychology Today says; "Optimists have a tendency to make lemonade out of lemons, and to then see the glass as half-full when it's half-empty. It's an admirable quality, one that can positively affect mental and physical health." Scheier & Carver (1985) define optimism as a general tendency to expect good outcomes, and found positive correlations with optimism and good physical health and more effective immune functioning. Carver (2005) found that optimism helps people deal with breast cancer. All the research on the subject seems to indicate that optimists "cope with stress in more adaptive ways than pessimists" (Nes & Segerstrom, 2006), and are more likely to engage in action-orientated problem-focused coping, more willing to seek social support, and more likely to emphasize the positive in their appraisal of stressful events - compared to the pessimist who is more likely to deal with stress by giving up, engaging in denial or wishful thinking (Weiten, 2010).

> *"A pessimist is one who makes difficulties of his opportunities and an optimist is one who makes opportunities of his difficulties." - Harry S. Truman*

There must be a reason for pessimism - or as some call it - realism. Although I consider myself an optimist, I have certainly experienced my fair share of cynicism, lack of faith in the human race, and "why do I bother" moments - however they pass. With the pessimist, I presume they linger. That - to me - is a one-way ticket to depression. However without some levels of pessimism – whether it be from a "down to earth" friend or a blunt partner - I could find myself floating up into the realms of borderline delusion if kept unchecked.

So my ongoing question is this, at what point does optimism stop and delusion begin? Perhaps when being overly optimistic stops being realistic, when this attitude begins to indicate neglect, defying the laws of physics, or just plain stupid? This reminds me of the old philosophical debate about good only being able to exist as long as there is evil - and furthermore - if there was no evil - good would lose its meaning. The yin and yang. If left unchecked, "evil" can do some terrible things - however acts done in the name of "good" can be equally unbalanced.

I haven't answered my question; however, I have come to a different conclusion; in order for optimism to exist there must be pessimists, and vice versa. Perhaps delusions come into play when there is not enough pessimism to ground the eternal optimist..? Food for thought...

Subtle Expression

The full expression of happiness includes these features: raised cheeks and the pulling up of the lip corners. One of these occurring individually could be a subtle sign of happiness.

1) Raising the cheeks by themselves can be a sign of subtle happiness, unless it is accompanied by a frown and / or the tightening of the eyes. This could then be considered a wince. Also as you can see with the mouth only smile, there is little to no difference in the eyes. This could also be noticed in very subtle sadness.

2) Pulling up the lip corners alone still creates the idea of a smile; however, without the raising of the cheeks it is likely to be a social smile (I prefer the term "social" to "fake"). If the smile is asymmetrical then it is likely that the expression is displaying contempt. Another

common sign of a social smile - and occasionally a contemptuous one - is what I refer to as "the dimpler" smile. This smile activates AU 14 instead of 12, where this action tightens the corners of the mouth, may cause a dimple or a bulge at the lip corners, and can sometimes curl the lip corners up (making it appear like a smile). One sided; the dimpler shows quite obvious contempt.

Masking and Social Smiles

A masking smile is an attempt to cover or hide another emotion, such as sadness, disgust or anger, with a smile – hence – placing a "mask" over the felt emotion. For example, this could occur when a person is feeling upset and does not want to show their sadness. They may wish to appear strong (as they may see their upset as a weakness), or "put on a brave face" in order to keep other people happy or to avoid questioning about what has caused the upset, or this could be a semi-permanent mask over someone feeling depressed or even hiding suicidal thoughts.

> **Tip:** A masking smile is a social smile covering another felt emotion. Remember not to jump to conclusions as to why the person is covering their emotion. Also, start becoming more aware of your own face and your own smiles when you greet people in the street, at home or in the office. What smile are *you* wearing?

Social smiles tend to be the most common smiles you will see during your day. These smiles exclude the activation of the *orbicularis oculi* (AU6), and only engage the *zygomaticus major* (lip corner puller or AU12), the sharp lip puller (AU13) or the dimpler (AU14) muscles.

 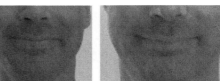

Lip Corner Puller (AU12)   Sharp Lip Puller (AU13)   Dimpler (AU14)

"We think of our face as reflecting our internal emotions, but that linkage works both ways - we can change our emotional state by altering our facial expression! Pasting a smile on your face, even if you are consciously faking it, can improve your mood and reduce stress." - Roger Dooley

Tip: Genuine versus polite smiles

Learning to pick polite smiles from genuine smiles takes a little work. Thankfully there are a few online resources that can help! Keeping in mind that websites update and url's change, I've also included the Google search term just in case. The first one that I recommend is the BBC "Spot The Fake Smile":
http://www.bbc.co.uk/science/humanbody/mind/surveys/smiles/

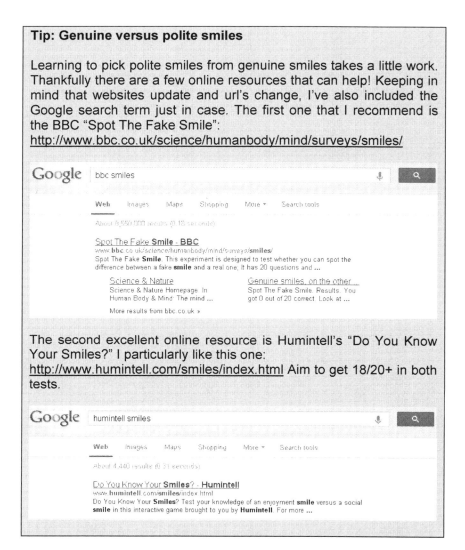

The second excellent online resource is Humintell's "Do You Know Your Smiles?" I particularly like this one:
http://www.humintell.com/smiles/index.html Aim to get 18/20+ in both tests.

Ranges in Emotion

Robert Plutchik's Wheel of Emotions places the range of happiness from mild to extreme as follows:

HAPPINESS		
Mild	**Medium**	**Extreme**
Serenity	Joy	Ecstasy

In my opinion, it helps to fully understand the emotion by exploring the range in more detail. So here are several more terms that fit under the happiness umbrella:

Amused, euphoric, blissful, elated, delighted, jubilant, glad, pleased

Where would you fit these other descriptions on the scale below?

Mild	Medium	Extreme
Serenity	Joy	Ecstasy

Genuine Smiles in Business

I've lost count how many times I've opened a local newspaper, viewed a billboard or witnessed a television advertisement and been affronted with a person's insincere fake smile - or worse - their genuine contempt in the form of a one-sided smile. As Connie Stevens said; "Nothing you wear is more important than your smile." And in making a good impression for your company, products and services, isn't it worth your while to make the effort with your smile?

A [genuine] smile is the best makeup that any girl can wear

One of the largest proportions of people's faces to advertising is the real estate industry. We want to see the face of the person who we will trust to sell our homes for us - or whom we wish to purchase from. However - perhaps because these images are in abundance - there are so many that should have left their faces off. The clenched teeth forced smile doesn't give me the impression of someone who would look after me. The contemptuous smirk image from the sales person who sees people as just a sale rather than a long-term customer. The stunned look of someone who appears shocked that their photo was just taken, who then thinks it a great idea to use this image on their marketing material... The list goes on. If you don't believe me, look to your local newspapers for proof.

Genuine smiles engage the zygomatic major muscle, which resides in the cheeks. This muscle tugs the lips upward, while the orbicularis oculi - the muscle which encircles the eye socket - squeezes the outside corners into the shape of a crow's foot. Other muscles can simulate a smile, but only the combination of the zygomatic major and the orbicularis oculi produces the genuine expression of a real smile, called the "Duchenne smile". The name came from French anatomist Guillaume Duchenne, who studied emotional expression by stimulating various facial muscles with electrical currents. In his

1862 book *Mecanisme de la Physionomie Humaine*, Duchenne wrote that the zygomatic major can be willed into action, but that only the "sweet emotions of the soul" forces the orbicularis oculi to contract. "Its inertia, in smiling," Duchenne wrote, "unmasks a false friend."

A natural smile produces wrinkles around the eyes whereas social smiles only engages the mouth

Genuine smiles are generated by the unconscious brain, which means they are automatic. To attempt to fake this process, photographers will ask you to say "Cheese", as this word pulls back the zygomatic major muscles. This however leaves an insincere-looking smile, which is why some of the best portrait photographers will try to make you laugh - creating a sincere smile.
So my advice is, if you are ever going to advertise anything that will include your face, do one of two things: 1) Think of something that will have you laugh a little, chuckle genuinely, and take a few photos so you have a choice. Select the one that looks the most genuine, the most natural. Or... 2) wear a neutral expression if you can't make a natural genuine smile or a neutral expression if this best suits your personality or advertising.

If you're unsure about an image you have and what message it may portray, feel free to contact us and ask - it's important that you put your best face forward! And remember what Judith Guest said; "People who keep stiff upper lips find that it's damn hard to smile."

CHAPTER 4
Surprise

"In a moment surprise passes as we figure out what is happening, and then surprise merges into fear, amusement, relief, anger, disgust, and so forth...or no emotion at all"
- Dr. Paul Ekman

Introduction

Surprise is the briefest of emotions, with a sudden onset that dissipates quickly as the stimulus that caused the surprise is understood. Once the event that caused the surprise has been evaluated, another emotion quickly follows, such as happiness (a pleasant surprise), fear (a frightening event that was surprising), or disgust (discovering a dead rodent under some rubbish) etc. The only time surprise will continue for longer than a few seconds is when further surprising stimulus occurs, although technically this becomes a separate surprise event.

> **Tip:** If someone's surprise lasts longer than a second or two, they're likely to be faking their surprise.

Paul Ekman refers to two triggers for surprise; *unexpected* and *misexpected* events. An unexpected event is stimulus that – as it states – is unexpected. Therefore genuine surprise can not result from anything that is expected, presumed, supposed, or anticipated in any way. Misexpected surprise can however occur when, say, you're expecting a friend to knock on your door – and when you answer it – you find it's a salesperson. Due to expecting one thing, the misexpected event causes surprise when another occurs (Ekman & Friesen, 2003). Matsumoto & Hwang sum up Larazus's (1991) trigger for surprise being "sudden novel objects", and the function of surprise being to help orient and obtain more information (Matsumoto & Hwang, 2012).

Appearance

As I've continued to teach people all around the world about facial expressions, I've noticed that a lot of people starting out learning about the seven universal expressions of emotion have issues noting the difference between surprise and fear – particularly as surprise does not last long, and usually merges into another emotion within several seconds (often fear).

The appearance of surprise consists of three main parts: raised eyebrows, raised eyelids, and the dropping of the jaw.

FACS Codes

Most Common FACS Codes for: Surprise - Action Units (AU's) 1+2+5+25+26	
AU1: Raising of the inner brow	AU2: Raising of the outer brow
AU5: Lifting of the eyelids	AU25: Lips apart
AU26: Lowering of the jaw	

Raised Eyebrows

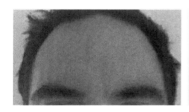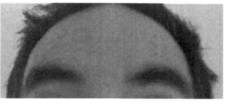

The raising of the eyebrows (Action Units 1+2) usually produces long horizontal wrinkles across the forehead, although often young children and some adults do not show these wrinkles. Included in this category are individuals who have Botox injected in their foreheads – could make for a good poker face. There are also people who already have quite pronounced deep wrinkles permanently etched across their forehead. In the instances where there are permanent wrinkles in an individual's neutral face, the horizontal creases will deepen and become more obvious when the eyebrows are raised.

Tip: It is quite normal for people to raise both the tone of their voice and their eyebrows when asking a question.

Raised Eyelids

The eyes open wide during surprise due to the raising of the upper eyelids (Action Unit 5). The sclera (whites of the eyes) are more visible – especially above the iris (the coloured part of the eye) – and occasionally below the iris. When the upper eyelids are lifted along with the eyebrows (1+2+5), more sclera is visible.

Dropping of the Jaw

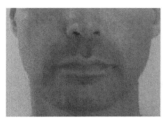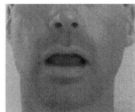

During surprise, the jaw relaxes and can drop (Action Unit 26), which causes the lips to part (Action Unit 25).

Tip: Fear and surprise are notoriously challenging to tell apart at times. Here are a few tips for helping you identify the differences.

Surprise raises the eyebrows and lifts the eyelids (FACS Codes 1+2+5). Often there is the opening of the mouth. Surprise will also turn into another emotion as the situation is understood – in other words – is it a good surprise (such as a birthday party or visit from a relative)? It could be sad surprise (such as being told of someone's death)? Disgust could follow after surprise (such as at first being surprised to find an animal previously chewed on by the cat, followed by disgust). As another example, surprise can also turn into fear as we realise we may be in danger. Surprise is the initial reaction, until our brains work out the meaning of the surprise.

Surprise   **Fear**

Fear is signified by (the FACS codes) 1+2+4+5, which is the raising of the complete eyebrows (1+2), and then lowering of the brows (4) which creates a push / pull, and finally (5) raise eyelids. There could also be mouth movements (such as the lip stretch AU20). The major difference between fear and surprise is the brow lowering (AU4) which fights against the raised lids (AU5).

It's in the eyes. I normally describe that the eyes in surprise are "softer", whereas the eyes in fear are much "harsher". The difference is surprise does not have the brow lowering.

Surprise   **Fear**

Subtle Expression

As discussed above, the full expression of surprise includes these features: the raised eyebrows and raised eyelids, and quite often the dropping of the jaw. One of these features occurring individually could be a subtle sign of surprise; however each can also have their own meaning.

1) By themselves, just raising the eyebrows can be a sign of interest, and is often used in normal conversations (along with the eyebrows) as punctuators and to emphasize points.
2) Raising the eyelids alone does not usually last long. By itself it can be a sign of interest, and is often used in normal conversations (along with the eyebrows) as punctuators and to emphasize points.
3) Dropping the jaw with no other facial expression can indicate being astonished or speechless (Ekman & Friesen, 2003, call this "dumbfounded"). Doing this intentionally as a facial emblem usually infers that the person wants to mock being astonished or speechless.

An occurrence of any of the signs of surprise could be subtle surprise. When you practice recognising surprise facial expressions, try to also take into account whether someone is using speech emblems or making a mock expression intentionally.

Ranges in Emotion

Robert Plutchik's Wheel of Emotions places the range of surprise from mild to extreme as follows:

SURPRISE		
Mild	**Medium**	**Extreme**
Distracted	Surprise	Amazement

Based upon this description, someone being mildly distracted fits into the category of surprise. I would suggest that this is the case initially, until it is determined what is causing the distraction. If you are distracted by something, your mild distraction may then become happiness when you realise it is a family member gently gaining your attention by doing something funny. However if the distraction came in the form of something more unpleasant – or even if you were very busy and didn't have time for distractions – then anger could follow.

In my opinion, it helps to fully understand the emotion by exploring the range in more detail. So here are several more terms that fit under the surprise umbrella:

Astonished, astounded, in awe, bewildered, to have an epiphany, shocked, startled, full of wonder.

Where would you fit these other descriptions on the scale below?

Mild	Medium	Extreme
Distracted	Surprise	Amazement

E.g.: Distracted is first, perhaps startled would come next, followed by bewildered etc. There's no perfect answer as so many definitions are subjective. This is to help you understand the scale of surprise.

CHAPTER 5
Contempt

"Contempt is only experienced about people or the actions of people." - Dr. Paul Ekman

Introduction

The feel of contempt is individual and based upon someone's personal morals. Someone can feel contemptuous towards another person when they feel they have the higher moral ground such as if the person is doing something that they morally disapprove of. The feeling of contempt often accompanies the inclination to raise the chin, which is where the term "looking down your nose" comes from. Contempt could be felt towards the show off, someone that does not hold the door open for a person in a wheelchair (if not anger), the absent person who is always late, the person that spits on the pavement (if not disgust), or even the person that did not apparently have to work hard to achieve success. Contempt can also be aimed internally, with self contempt being triggered by thoughts such as "I should have done better," "I forgot *again*," "I *knew* I was right the first time," "Should've guessed this was going to happen," and "Serves me right for keeping my hopes up," for example.

Contempt and disgust are closely related, with the key differences being disgust is experienced through taste, smell, sight or touch and contempt is experienced by feeling superior towards others or through self-disdain.

Tip: Research by Gottman, Coan, Carrere & Swanson (1998) found that wives whose husbands displayed contempt believed that their marital issues were severe, were un-reconcilable, and that they became ill regularly the longer it continued. The same study showed that this didn't occur with husbands that displayed anger or disgust.

Gottman, J. M., Coan, J., Carrere, S. & Swanson, C. (1998). *Journal of Marriage and Family.* 60 (1), 5-22. National Council on Family Relations

Matsumoto & Hwang sum up Larazus's (1991) trigger for contempt being "immoral actions", and the function of contempt being to assert superiority (Matsumoto & Hwang, 2012).

Appearance

The appearance of contempt is in the mouth. The appearance of a half-smile (often seen by Hollywood actors on the red carpet)

displays contempt. Someone can appear to be smiling fully, however if one side is stronger than the other (compared to their normal symmetrical smile), then it is likely contempt.

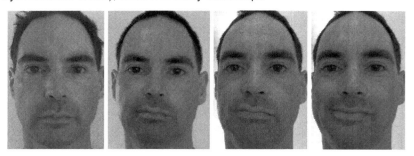

The appearance of contempt consists of an asymmetrical smile made up of one (or more than one) of the following: unilateral upper lip raise, one sided lip corner raise, or the asymmetrical tightening of a lip corner.

FACS Codes

Most Common FACS Codes for: Contempt – Asymmetrical Action Units (AU's) 10, 12 or 14	
Left/Right AU10: Upper lip raiser	Left/Right AU12: Raising of the lip corner
Left/Right AU14: Dimpler	

One-Sided Upper Lip Raise

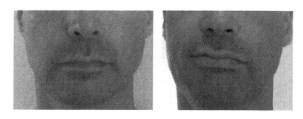

The raising of one side of the upper lip (Left or Right Action Unit 10) can create - depending on the intensity - a sneer-like contempt that deepens the nasolabial furrow (the diagonal creases beside the nose) on that side. This particular contempt virtually became signature smiles and singing styles for Elvis Presley and Billy Idol.

> **Tip:** Contempt is only experienced about people or the actions of people.

One-Sided Lip Corner Puller

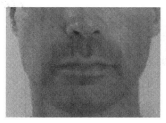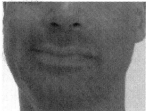

An asymmetrical lip corner puller (Left / Right AU 12) is the common half-smile, which can also occur when a smile is an expected response, however, it is not felt. An example could be listening to someone telling a sexist or racist joke where it may be inappropriate to respond overtly negative, so an insincere half-smile of contempt is the next best thing.

Tip: Disgust is experienced through taste, smell, sight or touch. Contempt is experienced by feeling superior towards others or self-disdain.

One-Sided Dimpler

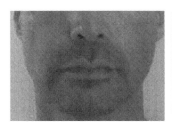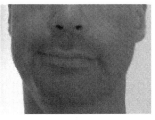

As mentioned briefly in Chapter 3, the tightening of the lip corners (AU14) is a common social smile, and often a contemptuous one - that I call the dimpler smile. This smile activates AU 14 instead of 12, where this action tightens the corners of the mouth, may cause a dimple or a bulge at the lip corners, and can sometimes curl the lip corners up (making it appear like a smile). The dimpler on one side (Left / Right AU14) is unmistakeable contempt.

Subtle Expression

As far as I am concerned, there is no subtle contempt – only intensity levels of contempt. It is either present or it is not, and it shows one side of the face stronger than the other. Contempt is the only genuine emotion that appears asymmetrical – all other genuine emotions appear symmetrical. The exceptions to this rule are stroke victims and people with partial facial paralysis, some learnt behaviour, and people born with their own idiosyncrasies. This is also why you should not jump to conclusions if you do not know the person's normal behaviour - does the person smile asymmetrically when they are smiling genuinely?

Ranges in Emotion

Robert Plutchik's Wheel of Emotions places contempt in between anger and disgust, so I have merged the two.

CONTEMPT		
Mild	**Medium**	**Extreme**
Disdain	Contempt	Arrogant Condescension

Here are several more terms that fit under the contempt umbrella:

Scornful, superior, despicable, immoral.

Where would you fit these other descriptions on the scale below?

Mild	Medium	Extreme
Disdain	Contempt	Arrogant Condescension

CHAPTER 6
Sadness

"Worry is a misuse of imagination." - Dan Zadra

Introduction

Someone is usually sad due to some kind of loss, whether it's a lost opportunity, loss of health, rejection or death of someone close, etc. Along with loss, sadness also follows pain (including the pain of romantic loss), disappointment and the feeling of hopelessness, and empathy is a way that we can also be sad *for* someone else. Sadness is one of the longer-lasting emotions as it generally lasts for hours or days. A sad mood could be someone who is feeling blue, the personality of someone sad would be considered melancholic, and long-term sadness would likely be termed as depression. Ekman & Friesen (2003) refers to a subcategory of sadness being *distress*.

Distress can be triggered by any of the examples above, and usually involves loud active suffering as a form of coping before sadness follows. While in a distressed state (which can include shock and anger blended with distress), loud crying and anger at the cause of the distress can occur, slowly subsiding into a feeling of hopelessness (if the circumstances or cause of the distress can not be corrected). Sadness follows after distress, with the possibility that triggers such as memories, actions or smells could re-invigorate the distress and cycle back around again.

Depression: Getting Through

Depression is a real problem, with an estimate of 15% of the population from high income countries (compared to 11% of low / middle income countries) experiencing some form of depression throughout their lifetime – and women being twice as likely to become depressed as men. (Source: *Science Daily.com)

In my opinion, depression is a longer-lasting emotional state that one either consciously or unconsciously sinks into, and I believe that in most cases emotional states can be changed quickly through three steps:

1) Changing your mental state. Be aware and take control of your own thoughts. When you're in a depressed state, unhappy memories are easier to access, so deliberately think of happy thoughts to break the vicious cycle.

---

2) Change your posture. There are a lot of studies that support that body language is linked to our emotions and states. Slouch with your head down and shoulders hunched will most likely create an emotional state that is negative and tired. Sit up, shoulders back and chin high will create quite a different attitude. Amy Cuddy says in one of her talks on power postures; "Our bodies change our minds, our minds change our behaviour and our behaviour changes our outcomes." Also become aware of your facial expressions. Smile – even if you don't mean it – as your brain may not catch on that you're faking your smile and your state may lift.

3) Change your language. Similar to #1, become aware and change the words you say both to yourself and out loud.

4) Move! I think exercising is a great way to feel better, plus it releases endorphins which trigger positive feelings in the body.

* Science Daily – *Global depression statistics*. Retrieved from http://www.sciencedaily.com/releases/2011/07/110725202240.htm

Matsumoto & Hwang sum up Larazus's (1991) triggers for sadness as the "loss of a loved one or object", and the function of sadness being to recoup resources or to call for help (Matsumoto & Hwang, 2012). Ekman agrees by saying; "The message of the sadness signal is a cry for help" (Ekman, 2003).

Appearance

Genuine sadness is most reliably identified with the raising of the inner eyebrow and lowering the brows, creating an arch-shaped eyebrow / \. As this eyebrow movement can be challenging to imitate / mimic, it's regularly missing from an actor's repertoire.

On Screen Emotions

As an unfortunate side effect of years of examining facial expressions I've become quite critical of what I can only describe as poor acting. As much as I love watching certain TV series, it ruins it for me to see, for example, someone being attacked who is not actually showing fear, a touching sad moment during a movie where the actor merely frowns rather than expresses sadness - and in particular - where an actor attempts to demonstrate real loss / grief / despair. In saying that, convincing happiness is also alarmingly absent in many television programs - and regularly in high-budget movies. I cringed when I watched Toby Maguire's "distress" in *Spiderman 2*, where he only frowned and raised his chin boss, resulting in a strange sort of smiling frown. Surely it would be worth their while hiring an emotional / FACS specialist to scan the material before things are immortalised on screen..?

With this in mind, television programs such as *Lie to Me* appeared to force actors to physically express the most correct and genuine expressions they could – as that was the focus of the series. And then there's *Dexter*. As a *Dexter* fan, I've been really impressed with Jennifer Carpenter's acting – who played the character "Debra Morgan". I thought that one clip in particular demonstrates such genuine agony and grief – coming from an actress who truly throws herself right into the role. Another example is Claire Danes who played "Carrie Mathson" on *Homeland*. Claire says; "In my personal life, I have plenty of vanity, but onscreen I'm not representing myself. I'm representing the person I'm playing." In my opinion, actors like these are few and far between, and fall into the category of great actors; actors such as Al Pacino, Jack Nicholson, Robert De Niro, Sean Connery, Meryl Streep and Natalie Portman – just to name a few.

The appearance of sadness consists of three main parts: raised inner corners of the eyebrows, lowering of the eyebrows, and the lowering of the lip corners. Additional signs of sadness can include the raising of the cheeks (which raises the lower eyelids) which portrays greater sadness, and the deepening of the nasolabial furrow can be a sign of holding back emotion or fighting back tears. Accompanying sadness can also include the lowering of the eyes and head, as well as the raising of the chin boss.

Tip: Sadness can blend with all emotions, however it's seen more commonly with fear and anger.

Most Common FACS Codes for: Sadness – Action Units (AU's) 1+4+15 (6, 11, 17)	
AU1: Raising of the inner brow	AU4: Lowering of the eyebrows
AU15: Lip corner depressor	
Additional Codes	
AU6: Raising of the cheeks	AU11: Deepening of the nasolabial furrow
AU17: Chin raiser	

Raised the Inner Brow and Lowering of the Brow

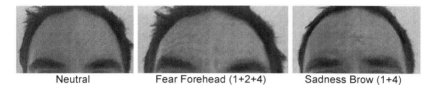

Neutral   Fear Forehead (1+2+4)   Sadness Brow (1+4)

The raising of the inner brow and lowering of the brow (Action Units 1+4) create the / \ arch known as the sadness brow. This differs from the Fear Forehead / Brow (covered in detail in the next chapter), as sadness only raises the inner corner of the eyebrows (Action Unit 1) rather than the full eyebrows (Action Units 1+2). The horizontal wrinkles tend to curve or bunch above the glabella (area of skin in between and just above the eyebrows), which is a fairly reliable sign of sadness.

Tip: The most reliable facial indicator of sadness is the raising of the inner corners only of the eyebrows (referred to as AU 1 in FACS). Not many people can do this intentionally, hence as I mentioned above, I wince at some actors' attempts at sadness. Even my attempt at sadness above doesn't really capture the "sadness brow", so I've attached another genuine sadness brow below, that clearly shows the inner brows pushing up against the lowering of the brow.

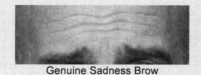

Genuine Sadness Brow

Lip Corner Depressor

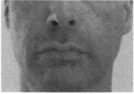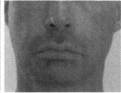

The lip corner depressor (Action Unit 15) is – in my opinion – how most people would signal sadness without actually feeling the emotion. I find that fake sadness is also often accompanied by the raising of the chin boss (Action Unit 17), particularly with children. The pulling of the muscles works in virtually the opposite direction to the smile (Action Unit 12), and changes the shape of the lips so they are – as the name suggests – pulled down at the corners and the lower lip is usually stretched horizontally.

Tip: When the lip corner depressor (AU15) is pulled down quite far it can give the impression that the face has grown longer. Hence the term; "Why the long face?" is really asking; "Why do you look so sad?"

Also, the combination of AU15+17 can give the impression of a pout rather than sadness, particularly with children (when there's an absence of the oblique sadness eyebrows). This can also represent a mouth shrug, which carries the same meaning as a shoulder shrug.

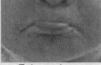

Fake sadness

Subtle Expression

As discussed above, the full expression of sadness includes these features: the raised inner corners of the eyebrows, lowering of the eyebrows, and the lowering of the lip corners. In addition there are several other signs of sadness that can be detected. One of these occurring individually could be a subtle sign of sadness.

1) By themselves, just raising the inner corner of the eyebrows is usually a reliable sign of sadness (or even empathy), which is made stronger by the presence of the brow lowering. In some instances

however this can be used in conversation as punctuators, similar to the raising of the eyebrows.

2) Lowering the lip corners by themselves can indicate a want to portray sadness, however is unlikely to be genuine sadness with this action alone.

3) Lowering the brows into a frown by themselves is unlikely to signify sadness. It could indicate concentration, attempting to see something clearly and / or blocking out bright light, and it could also signify irritation and anger.

4) Raising the cheeks by themselves can be a sign of subtle happiness, unless it is accompanied by a frown and / or the tightening of the eyes. This could then be considered a wince. This could also be noticed in very subtle sadness.

5) The deepening of the nasolabial furrow can be a sign of holding back emotion or fighting back tears.

> **Tip:** The deepening of the nasolabial furrow (AU11 – the diagonal creases beside the nose) can be a sign of holding back emotion or fighting back tears. This is different from disgust which wrinkles the nose (AU9) or raises the top lip (AU10) – both actions may subsequently deepen the nasolabial furrow; however that is as a result rather than the source.

6) The lowering of the eyes and head can mean anything out of context, from sadness to deep thinking. This is not a reliable indicator of subtle sadness.

7) The raising of the chin boss can often be used as a punctuator to tell the other person they are listening. By itself it can be a sign of sadness or disgust, however it could also indicate thought, being impressed, empathetic, or fake sadness amongst other possible interpretations.

8) One last subtle sign of sadness is the bottom lip can tremble with some individuals.

When you practice recognising sadness facial expressions, look to the eyebrows first.

> ## Predicting Suicide from Facial Expressions
>
> Heller & Haynal (1994) used the Facial Action Coding System to study the facial expressions of patients who were grouped into three groups: diagnosed with depression, patients who attempted suicide, and patients who reattempted suicide a year later.
>
> The study revealed that suicidal depressive patients didn't use their upper face nearly as much as non-suicidal depressed patients. This suggests that the decrease in upper face movement may be due to

the patients' intent to refrain from communication with others - the raising of the eyebrows is a common verbal punctuator, used to show interest and to emphasis points.

Heller, M., & Haynal, V. (1994). Depression and suicide faces. *Cahiers Psychiatriques Genevois, 16*, 107-117.

Ranges in Emotion

Robert Plutchik's Wheel of Emotions places the range of sadness from mild to extreme as follows:

SADNESS		
Mild	**Medium**	**Extreme**
Pensiveness	Sadness	Grief

Here are several more terms that fit under the sadness umbrella:

Depression, unhappiness, misery, melancholic, gloomy, in despair.

Where would you fit these other descriptions on the scale below?

Mild	Medium	Extreme
Pensiveness	Sadness	Grief

6 Basic Human Needs (Tony Robbins, Personal Power II)

According to Tony Robbins, we human beings have six basic needs in order to survive in this world. How happy are you in these areas?

1) Certainty: All human beings crave a certain level of safety, assurance and predictability in our lives, for this is the foundation of our most basic behaviour: survival. Long-term uncertainty can be rather trying…

2. Variety: We all need a change of scenery every now and then, watch a new movie, travel to a new country. Too much uncertainty generates fear, while not enough causes boredom. Find a balance between certainty and variety that suits you.

3. Significance: We all need to feel important, unique, and special. That feeling of not mattering to anyone can be very damaging.

4. Connection: Relationships are an extremely important part of our lives, whether they are intimate, family, friends or business colleagues. However if we're too busy being significant in this world, we may forget who our greatest supporters are.
Find a balance between significance and connection that suits your situation.

5. Growth: Tony suggests that everything is either growing or dying; one or the other. In order to stay in the growing stage we need something to strive for, a goal, something that'll challenge us to grow and take our lives to the next level. All too often I've witnessed people retiring and dying not long afterwards – they lost their purpose.

6. Contribution: This can be summed up as giving back in some way, shape or form.

CHAPTER 7
Fear

"Everything you want is on the other side of fear."
- Jack Canfield

Introduction

Fear is triggered by injury. This injury could be physical, psychological, or both. Fear can also be triggered in anticipation of any kind of pain, or while actually feeling pain. This is better described with examples: fear can be caused by anticipating physical pain (such as waiting at the dentist to receive a filling) or by anticipating psychological pain (having to make an unprepared public speech). Fear can also be triggered by being hurt physically (being badly cut) or by being hurt psychologically (such as being rejected by a lover).

SDL FEAR MATRIX

	Physical Harm	Psychological Harm
Anticipated Harm	Waiting at the Dentist	Making a speech
Actual Harm	Receiving a deep cut	Being rejected by a loved one

The Fear Matrix helps to illustrate how fear can be triggered through physical or psychological harm, and the relationship between actual and anticipated harm.

It is quite possible to be both physically and psychologically injured at the same time, for example, Ekman & Friesen (2003) suggest this may be the case if a teenager is beaten up in front of his girlfriend, as this would bruise both the body and self-esteem.

Often surprise precedes fear, and fear can quickly shift or blend into other emotions. Matsumoto & Hwang sum up Larazus's (1991) trigger for fear as the "threat to physical or emotional well-being", and the function of fear being to avoid threat and reduce harm (Matsumoto & Hwang, 2012).

Phobias

Phobia comes from the Greek word phóbos, which means "morbid fear". In psychological terms, phobias are generally classified as anxiety disorders in regards to something in particular. The most common phobias are: Arachnophobia (fear of spiders), Ophidiophobia (fear of snakes), Acrophobia (fear of heights), Agoraphobia (fear of social situations where escape is difficult) and Cynophobia (fear of dogs).*

In my opinion, the two major differences between phobias and fears come down to intensity (or acuteness) and perspective. Someone can have a fear of public speaking without having a "morbid fear" or phobia. Experiencing a phobia could be described as a state of extreme fear that can be paralyzing; however they are not normally based upon real threats (making them more illogical reactions). A fear of public speaking is more often than not a general fear of looking bad / making a mistake in front of an audience, however a person can still get up and speak as well as receive coaching and get better with practice and experience.

Some common fears (not phobias) include: fear of flying, public speaking, heights, the dark, intimacy, death, failure, rejection and commitment.**

* Psychology About.com - *Common Phobias - The Ten Most Common Phobias.* Retrieved from
http://psychology.about.com/od/phobias/p/commonphobias.htm
** Self Help Collective – *Top 10 Fears – List Of Fears.* Retrieved from
http://www.selfhelpcollective.com/top-10-fears.html

Appearance

Fear is characterised by the eyebrows and upper eyelids being raised, with the eyebrows being pulled down in opposition which draws the brows together. The mouth may stretch back, lips part and the jaw may drop.

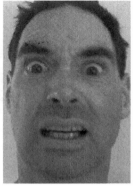

FACS Codes

Most Common FACS Codes for: Fear - Action Units (AU's) 1+2+4+5 (20, 25, 26)	
AU1: Raising of the inner brow	AU2: Raising of the outer brow
AU4: Lowering of the eyebrows	AU5: Lifting of the eyelids
Additional Codes	
AU20: Lip Stretch	AU25: Lips apart
AU26: Lowering of the jaw	

Litany Against Fear

"I must not fear. Fear is the mind-killer. Fear is the little-death that brings total obliteration. I will face my fear. I will permit it to pass over me and through me. And when it has gone past I will turn the inner eye to see its path. Where the fear has gone there will be nothing. Only I will remain."
- Bene Gesserit Litany Against Fear (from Frank Herbert's book, *Dune*).

Raised Eyebrows and Lowering of the Brow

Neutral   Surprise Brow   Fear Brow

The raising of the eyebrows (Action Units 1+2) alone can be seen in the surprise brow, however the addition of the brow lowering (Action Unit 4) can be seen in the fear brow, pulling the eyebrows down and together.

Raised Eyelids

Neutral   Surprise Eyes   Fear Eyes

The eyes open wide during fear due to the raising of the upper eyelids (Action Unit 5); however the eyes differ in appearance from surprise due to the lowering of the brow. I tend to describe the fear combination (4+5) as giving the eyes a much harsher look, as opposed to surprise where the eyes look much softer in comparison. Also as with surprise, the sclera (whites of the eyes) are more visible – especially above the iris (the coloured part of the eye).

Lip Stretch, Lips Part and Jaw Drop

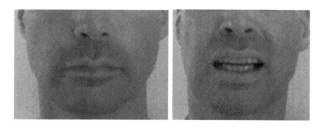

During fear, the mouth will often open (Lips Apart Action Unit 25 and Jaw Drop Action Unit 26) and pull the lips laterally back towards the ears; making what I call an "Ekk" looking mouth gesture (Action Unit 20). The lips are also tense in fear, where the lips are more relaxed in surprise.

Subtle Expression

As discussed above, the full expression of fear includes these features: eyebrows and upper eyelids being raised, with the eyebrows being pulled down in opposition which draws the brows together. The mouth may stretch back, lips part and the jaw may drop. One of these features occurring individually could be a subtle sign of fear; however they can also have their own meaning.

1) By themselves, just raising the eyebrows can be a sign of interest, and is often used in normal conversations (along with the eyebrows) as punctuators and to emphasize points.
2) Raising the eyelids alone does not usually last long. By itself it can be a sign of interest, and is often used in normal conversations (along with the eyebrows) as punctuators and to emphasize points. It can also be a good indicator of subtle fear.
3) Lowering the brows into a frown by themselves is unlikely to signify fear. It could indicate concentration, attempting to see something clearly and / or blocking out bright light, and it could also signify irritation and anger.
4) The mouth stretch by itself can be a very good indicator of fear. This mouth movement also occurs (generally as a micro expression) when there is just enough warning of something negative happening that surprise is not present, such as the creaking sound of a door alerting you that it is about to slam, or the fumble of a glass as it slips out of your fingers.

Turtling and Negative Anticipation

When we anticipate an unpleasant stimulus (using the examples above; the second or two before a door slams shut or the moment before a glass smashes on the floor) we tend to grimace. The grimace is usually made up of the mouth stretch, tightened of the eyes and turtling the neck – which is to turtle our necks down (almost like a bracing position) in expectation of the stimulus.

An occurrence of any of the signs of fear may or may not indicate subtle fear, as some facial gestures have multiple meanings. Always try to take into account the context of the situation; what just happened prior to seeing one of the fear cues? This is where analysing still images can be tricky – all we can do is note what we see within the context of the image.

Ranges in Emotion

Robert Plutchik's Wheel of Emotions places the range of fear from mild to extreme as follows:

FEAR		
Mild	**Medium**	**Extreme**
Apprehension	Fear	Terror

Here are several more terms that fit under the fear umbrella:

Distress, dread, tenseness, unease, worried, shyness, anxiety.

Where would you fit these other descriptions on the scale below?

Mild	Medium	Extreme
Apprehension	Fear	Terror

CHAPTER 8
Disgust

"It is not only tastes, smells, and touches, or the thought, sight, or sound of them that can bring forth disgust but also the actions and appearance of people, or even ideas"
- Dr. Paul Ekman

Introduction

The feeling of aversion, disliking and repugnance are all varying degrees of disgust. This emotion can be triggered through tasting something revolting (such as rotten food), an unpleasant smell (such as vomit), seeing something repulsive or offensive (such as recently burnt skin, or the behaviour of a parent scolding their child harshly) or through touch (such as leaning onto a sticky table). Disgust is felt by being physically present to the disgusting stimulus, as well as by imagining or recalling the disgusting stimulus.

> **Tip:** There are a lot of cultural differences as to what people consider disgusting, and in my opinion the largest discrepancies are in cultural cuisine. If anyone has watched reality television programs such as *The Amazing Race* and *Fear Factor* you'll be fully aware of this - I don't think I could ever stomach snake blood, duck foetus, bee larvae, spiders or bugs...

As mentioned in Chapter 5, disgust and contempt are closely related, with disgust being experienced by taste, smell, sight or touch and contempt being experienced in regards to feeling superior towards others or self-disdain. Matsumoto & Hwang sum up Larazus's (1991) trigger for disgust being "contamination or offensive rotten objects", and the function of disgust being repulsion or elimination of the contaminated object (Matsumoto & Hwang, 2012).

Appearance

The appearance of disgust consists mainly around the nose and mouth area. The deepening of the nasolabial furrow (the diagonal creases besides the nose) is a fairly reliable sign of disgust, which is done through wrinkling the nose, raising the upper lip, or a combination of both. Additional signs of disgust can include lowering of the lip corners, depressing of the lower lip, raising of the chin boss, and the opening of the mouth.

> **Tip:** Some people have deep creases along their nasolabial furrow in their neutral face, and can be mistaken for looking disgusted when they aren't – so always be aware of the person's neutral face to avoid these kinds of errors.

> **Tip:** Tears seem to be the only body fluid that doesn't evoke feelings of disgust.

FACS Codes

Most Common FACS Codes for: Disgust – Action Units (AU's) 9 & / or 10 (15,16,17,25,26)	
AU9: Nose wrinkler	AU10: Upper lip raiser
Additional Codes	
AU15: Lip corner depressor	AU16: Lower lip depressor
AU17: Chin raiser	AU25: Lips apart
AU26: Lowering of the jaw	

The Disgust Mouth and Nose

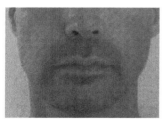 

Disgust will cause the nose to wrinkle (Action Unit 9), the upper lip to raise (AU10) – or a combination of both. The classic tell tale indicator of disgust is the deepening of the nasolabial furrow (the diagonal creases beside the nose), and is one of the easiest ways to distinguish disgust from anger (unless it's a blended expression of disgusted anger). Further signs of disgust could include the lowering of the lip corners (AU15), lowering of the bottom lip (AU16), raising of the chin boss (AU17) and opening of the mouth (lips parting AU25 and jaw drop AU26).

Often with disgust a frown is present, however most of the time the lowering of the brows is caused by the nose wrinkling.

> **Tip:** As mentioned in Chapter 6, the deepening of the nasolabial furrow (AU11) can be a sign of holding back emotion or fighting back tears. Disgust may subsequently deepen the nasolabial furrow; however that is as a result rather than the source. AU11 causes the deepening of the furrow, whereas AU9 & AU10 lift other muscles that result in the deepening of the furrow.

Subtle Expression

As discussed above, the full expression of disgust includes: the nose wrinkling, raising of the upper lip, or a combination of both. In addition there are several other signs of disgust that can be detected – one of these occurring individually could be a subtle sign of disgust.

1) By themselves, either the nose wrinkler or upper lip raise still sends the message of disgust. This could also be a facial gesture indicating disgust, used to indicate something unpleasant.
2) Lowering the lip corners by themselves can indicate a want to portray sadness.
3) Depressing the lower lip by itself can indicate disgust as it's not used as a common facial emblem or punctuator.
4) The raising of the chin boss can often be used as a punctuator to tell the other person they are listening. By itself it can be a sign of sadness or disgust, however it could also indicate thought, being impressed, empathetic, or fake sadness amongst other possible interpretations.

> ### Frozen-Affect Expressors
>
> I've come across several professional models who intentionally wear a sort of disgust-sneer-smile as their modelling face. Based upon Ekman & Friesen's (2003) work on facial expressors, I'd class this example as the models being frozen-affect expressors: traces of another emotion remain on some part of their face, even when they're not feeling any emotion. Why do some people do this?

Perhaps its genetics or muscle memory - however people who are frozen-affect expressors are usually oblivious to it.

Ranges in Emotion

Robert Plutchik's Wheel of Emotions places the range of disgust from mild to extreme as follows:

DISGUST		
Mild	**Medium**	**Extreme**
Boredom	Disgust	Loathing

Here are several more terms that fit under the disgust umbrella:

Abhorrence, dislike, distaste, hate, revulsion, nausea, objection.

Where would you fit these other descriptions on the scale below?

Mild	Medium	Extreme
Boredom	Disgust	Loathing

Blended Emotions

When I first started examining faces, learning micro expressions and trying to determine what emotions were present in an image or video, something found difficult was telling the difference between anger and disgust.

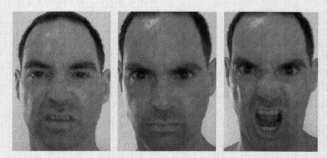

The main ingredients of anger (see Chapter 9 for more details on anger) include the lowering of the eyebrows (AU4), and the raising (AU5) and tightening (AU7) of the eyelids. This can also include any number of other factors such as clenching the jaw, gritting teeth or tightening the lips for example.

Disgust (as we've covered in this chapter) is recognised most by the wrinkling of the nose (AU9) or the raising of the upper lip (AU10). It's also common to see the raising of the chin boss (AU17) in disgust, and perhaps even the lower lip dropping (AU16).

This is where we come to an interesting question - what if there are signs of both anger *and* disgust in an image? It's easier to ascertain an expression from a video clip as you can actually see things in context, identify the muscles moving in what order, and get the whole picture. Well, my simple answer is this: there certainly *can* be blended emotions. Sometimes after people have gone through online micro expressions training or read a book on facial expressions they can take on a mindset of black and white, having the certainty that there must be only one answer - as that's what some training says.

However in reality this isn't the case. Masking smiles for example – what other emotion are they masking or hiding? Someone could be disgusted with a scene yet paste on a social smile. Someone may be sad however they cover their sadness with a smile to avoid being asked questions. Someone could be really angry yet trying to shake it off for the benefit of the people around them.

Blended emotions are everywhere.

CHAPTER 9
Anger

"For every minute you are angry you lose sixty seconds of happiness." - Ralph Waldo Emerson

Introduction

I think Elliott Larson sums up anger well in his quote, "Anger is only one letter short of danger." Anger can be evoked by any number of personalised triggers, with everyone having their own individual "pet hates", tolerances, and breaking points. Dr. Robert Anthony says; "The angry people are those who are most afraid," which I believe is true in some circumstances; however I don't believe this to be the case overall. Ekman & Friesen (2003) suggest that anger can be aroused in six different ways; *frustration*, *physical threat*, *psychological attack*, *moral violation*, *failure to meet expectations*, and *when anger is directed at you*. In my opinion, fear would only fit into a few of these categories.

> **Tip:** Even though anger is considered one of the most dangerous emotions, it can also serve as a motivator. Anger can motivate us to stop or change whatever is causing us to feel angry, as well as communicating with the autonomic nervous system in fight-or-flight situations.

Frustration: I believe frustration is the most common cause of anger, and is best described when something or someone interferes with the pursuit of a goal. The goal could be on any scale, from something small (such as going to the store only to find you forgot the most important item upon returning home) to something a little larger (such as breaking a limb just before sports try outs, purchasing a car to find it has mechanical issues, or finding out that an investment firm hasn't looked after your money). To some extent, anger acts to assist in removing the source of frustration. Also, what frustrates one person may not frustrate another.

> There are two things that particularly bother me; frustration and injustice. For me, frustration stems from feeling helpless, when I'm not in a position to change a negative situation. What's helped me here is adopting the attitude to some extend of "what will be, will be". Letting go of having to control every little detail has certainly helped me deal with frustration. Injustice is another beast; I can sympathise with the vigilante mindset, however (of course) I don't condone vigilantism!

Physical Threat: If someone poses a real physical threat, fear or a mixture of fear and anger would likely result. If the threat is more superficial or more evenly matched, then anger is likely to be triggered. Fight-or-flight.

> I started learning martial arts to improve my fitness and to learn how to defend myself. Something I didn't realise I was going to gain was self confidence, and it's self confidence that has had me avoid quite a number of confrontations. Depending on the mindset of the martial arts instructor and the student, I suggest that learning martial arts is an excellent preventative measure for avoiding physically threatening situations, and provides a much higher chance of walking away should an actual confrontation occur.

Psychological Attack: Anger can be triggered by insults, and any actions that leave someone feeling disrespected – which generally intensifies if the action is perceived as intentional. As each person's life experiences are different, an insult that causes anger and upset to one person may not when aimed at someone else. People's perceptions of respect and tolerance are individualised.

Moral Violation: Even though not directly involved, anger can be triggered by witnessing someone else being mistreated. Where each person's moral baseline differs for everyone, therefore some people wouldn't get angry witnessing domestic violence or public degrading of children. However, for a lot of people this would be too much to ignore, and a phone call to the police or social services would follow.

Failure to Meet Expectations: Most common as a parental reaction to children, impatience and irritation can occur when requested or expected tasks are not completed. This could be from the child not tidying up after themselves, to the husband who was expected to have the lawns mowed before guests arrive.

> I've been on the receiving end of the anger triggered by the failure to meet expectations at home a few times, mainly due to the expectations not being communicated. If you find yourself in this situation, taking the time to find out where the anger is coming from can save a lot of time and is much more productive than becoming angry in return.

When Anger Is Directed At You: Perhaps more so when there appears to be no valid justification to receive anger, some people reciprocate anger directed at them.

Depending of an individual's life, experience and history, virtually anything can trigger anger. Matsumoto & Hwang sum up Larazus's

(1991) trigger for anger being "goal obstruction, injustice and perceived norm violations", and the function of anger being to remove the obstacle (Matsumoto & Hwang, 2012).

Appearance

During anger, the eyebrows are pulled down and together, and the eyelids raise and tense to give the appearance of a harsh glare. Depending on the intensity of the anger, the lips may tighten, press together, or the jaw may clench. The mouth may also open – often accompanied with shouting or a yell. In addition, the upper lip and chin boss can rise in anger.

FACS Codes

Most Common FACS Codes for: Anger – Action Units (AU's) 4+5+7 (10+17+23+24+25+26)	
AU4: Lowering of the eyebrows	AU5: Lifting of the eyelids
AU7: Lid tightener	
Additional Codes	
AU10: Upper lip raiser	AU17: Chin raiser
AU23: Lip tightener	AU24: Lip presser
AU25: Lips apart	AU26: Lowering of the jaw

Anger Brow

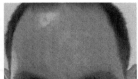

The lowering and drawing in of the eyebrows (AU4) creates the appearance of a frown. This looks different from sadness and fear as there are no other actions pulling against the lowering of the brow, and usually creates vertical wrinkles due to the bunching of skin around the glabella (area just above the root of the nose in between the eyebrows). Anger does not produce or deepen existing horizontal wrinkles across the forehead.

> **Tip:** Try to avoid mistaking the lowering of the brow alone as anger when it may be someone in a serious mood, thinking, or solving a puzzle etc. Take into account other potential signs of anger in the face, body language and environment. In my experience, someone being accused of being angry when they are not can in fact make them angry.

<u>Anger Eyes</u>

The eyes open wider during anger due to the raising of the upper eyelids (AU5), and the tensing of the eyelids (AU7) provides a harsher quality to the eyes. When mixed with AU4, the combination creates the appearance of a penetrating angry glare (4+5+7).

Subtle Expression

As discussed above, the full expression of anger includes these features: the eyebrows being pulled down and together, the eyelids raise and tense, and the lips may tighten, press together, or the jaw may clench. In addition, the upper lip and chin boss can rise in anger. Some of these signs by themselves could be a subtle sign of anger.

1) Lowering the brows alone could be a subtle sign of anger (more reliable with another sign of anger), however it can also display deep thinking, disapproval, or something as simple as shading the eyes from a bright light or the sun. Not a reliable sign of anger by itself.
2) Raising the eyelids alone does not usually last long. By itself it can be a sign of interest, and is often used in normal conversations (along with the eyebrows) as punctuators and to emphasize points.
3) Tensing of the eyes could be a sign of anger. Other potential meanings could include wincing in pain or even squinting to see something at a distance. Try to consider the environment and circumstances before assuming anger.
4) Raising the upper lip by itself sends the message of disgust. This could also be a facial gesture indicating disgust, used to indicate something unpleasant.

5) The raising of the chin boss can often be used as a punctuator to tell the other person they are listening. By itself it can be a sign of sadness or disgust, however it could also indicate thought, being impressed, empathetic, or fake sadness amongst other possible interpretations

6) Tensing of the lips – not to be mistaken as pursing the lips – can be a fairly reliable sign of anger, depending on the situation. Emotional arousal – positive or negative – can also tense the lips.

> **Tip:** The old term "keeping a stiff upper lip" generally signified holding back emotion or demonstrating self restraint, as a trembling upper lip (usually caused by fear or anger) was looked upon as a sign of weakness. The term is most often used to describe someone who does not demonstrate emotion.

7) Dropping the jaw with no other facial expression can indicate being astonished or speechless (Ekman & Friesen, 2003, call this "dumbfounded"). Doing this intentionally as a facial emblem usually infers that the person wants to mock being astonished or speechless.

8) I also want to add in here the jaw clenching. Visible signs of the jaw tightening can be a reliable indicator of anger beginning.

An occurrence of any of the signs of anger may or may not indicate subtle anger. Try to take into account the context of the situation.

Ranges in Emotion

Robert Plutchik's Wheel of Emotions places the range of anger from mild to extreme as follows:

ANGER		
Mild	**Medium**	**Extreme**
Annoyance	Anger	Rage

Here are several more terms that fit under the anger umbrella: **Fury, wrath, bitterness, loathing, resentment, hatred, frustration, exasperation, agitation, aggravation, grouchiness, irritation.**

Where would you fit these other descriptions on the scale below?

Mild	Medium	Extreme
Annoyance	Anger	Rage

PART 1 – WHAT ARE THESE EXPRESSIONS?

Review Part 1 and write down what you think these expressions might be. Keep in mind that there could also be a blend of emotions. Suggested answers can be found in the Appendix at the back of the book for these images.

Image 1

Image 2

Image 3

Image 4

Image 5 – FACS Codes included for this image

There are verified FACS codes for this image in the Appendix.

There are verified FACS codes for this image in the Appendix.

PART 2

GESTURES AND BODY LANGUAGE

CHAPTER 10
Gestures & Body Language: Hands and Arms

"As the tongue speaketh to the ear, so the gesture speaketh to the eye" - Sir Francis Bacon (1891)

Introduction

Over the last nine chapters we have covered facial expressions in some detail, which covers the first channel of communication. Over the next three chapters I will be introducing what I believe is all you will ever need to know about body language and gestures – with the exception of cultural differences. This chapter is an introduction to common gestures and body language using hands and arms. It is important to remember that body language has a sender *and* a receiver – therefore interpretation of any gestures can be subjective. Interpreting still images lacks the context surrounding the image therefore we can not accurately know what happened just prior to the photograph being taken, nor do we know anything about the situation. In my opinion most body language interpretations and information should be considered anecdotal, although some body language interpretations regarding deception are supported by research (such as speech illustrators). Another point is that the sender may not intend to portray a particular message; however the receiver may still unconsciously interpret the "message" a certain way. In my opinion, always use body language interpretations as guidelines rather than empirically-researched and scientifically-backed facts.

"Body language is an outward reflection of a person's emotional condition. Each gesture or movement can be a valuable key to an emotion a person may be feeling at the time."
- Allan Pease

A Common Issue with Body Language

One of the worst body language myths spread by body language "experts" is that specific actions or gestures have specific meanings. For example, Max folds his arms which means that Max is defensive or in a negative mood. I want to make this quite clear: **I will never say; "This action means that."** Max folds his arms. We have to take into account a lot more information before making an interpretation as to why Max has his arms folded; does Max fold his arms all the time (it is his normal behaviour or does Max hardly ever fold his arms)? What is the rest of Max's body saying (face, arms / hands and legs)? Of course – we must also take into account what the weather is like, as it may be due to the cold that Max is folding his arms.

Tip: Avoid assuming that one isolated gesture has a significant meaning without taking into account the context of the situation, along with a full analysis of the face and body. People can have quite differing opinions on body language interpretation. Interpreting body language is just that – an interpretation. Over time one becomes more accurate by gaining feedback and remembering not to assume a meaning e.g. taking in the whole scene / image / context, and not trying to guess what is happening. My advice is to come to a conclusion of an interpretation only after doing a complete mini-analysis of everyone in an image (if there's more than one person) which will include facial expressions, arm positions, any hand gestures and feet positions – and the body posture in relation to others. This works a little differently with video or live analysis, as the context of what is happening is much clearer.

One more piece of advice for all budding body language analysers: If you're not sure of an interpretation, say so. Don't be afraid to say that the gesture is too ambiguous to interpret, or list a number of "possible" interpretations, without claiming any as being "the answer".

The Mind / Body Connection

The "law of attraction" is the name given to the concept of "like attracts like" and that by focusing on positive or negative thoughts, one can bring about positive or negative results (Wikipedia). This perspective infers "what we think about, we bring about" and that there is a mind-body connection. I also believe there is a body-mind connection that works in reverse. Social psychologist Amy Cuddy says; "Our bodies change our minds, our minds change our behaviour and our behaviour changes our outcomes."

Body language affects how others see us as well as how we see and feel about ourselves, such as standing in a posture of confidence, even when we don't feel confident – can affect testosterone and cortisol levels in the brain (Cuddy, 2012)*. As I mentioned in Chapter 6, there studies in support of body language being linked to our emotional state. If you wrinkle your nose in disgust you may feel nauseous** just as smiling, even when you are not feeling happy can lift your mood. How we hold ourselves can even affect our memory:

studies have revealed that folding arms and legs while sitting in a lecture theatre can reduce recall of the information by up to 40% - another good reason to avoid folding your arms.

* You Tube - *Amy Cuddy: Your body language shapes who you are.* Retrieved from http://www.youtube.com/watch?v=Ks-_Mh1QhMc
** This experience was shared by Erika Rosenberg – international FACS instructor – when she demonstrates AU9 (nose wrinkler) and AU10 (upper lip raiser) for long periods of time.

"The body never lies." - Martha Graham

Hand Gestures

In this section I provide a number of common gestures accompanied with interpretations. Although these should only be used as guidelines, interpretations increase in credibility with more evidence, for example a tightly-clenched fist accompanied by an arm barrier and an angry facial expression provides three separate clues and increases the accuracy that the individual has a negative attitude.

> **Tip:** Always be careful analysing still images – in the majority of cases we view out of context. All we can do is interpret them the best we can while ensuring we state that they are in fact our interpretations.

There are more nerve connections between the brain and the hands than between any other part of the body, with studies analysing emotional cues from facial expressions and hand gestures revealing that hands provide insights to emotional states (Balomenos, Raouzaiou, Ioannou, Drosopoulos, Karpouzis, & Kollias 2005). "Hand talking" is used more by the Italians and French, whereas it is still uncommon to see the English waving their hands during a normal un-heated conversation.

> **Tip:** Most body language interpretations depend on the situation, environment and facial expressions.

While there are cultural differences in hand gestures, signals, meanings and interpretations, there are some common hand gestures you can become familiar with.

Here are some of the common hand gestures and signals:

Rubbing Palms Together

Rubbing the palms together often communicates positive expectations – you may see a gambler doing this with dice in the hope of winning. You may notice that a salesperson could do this in expectation of making a sale. This is also common for someone with cold hands! Anxiety is more often identified with "wringing" the hands, rolling / clasping them rather than just rubbing the palms together.

In saying this, each person is different, and not one interpretation is universal.

Did you know? Dr. Matsumoto suggests that covering one's face could be an evolutionary reaction to hide ones emotions from enemies.

Thumb & Finger Rub

This gesture is commonly used to indicate money, symbolizing the rubbing of a coin between the thumb and fingertips. In my opinion this is becoming rarer to see, and I think generally has a negative association about money – and should probably be avoided in any professional environments.

Did you know? When counting out positives and negatives, right handed people usually reserve their favoured points of view for their right hand, and left-handers favour their left for the positives.

Hands Clenched Together

The hands clenched gesture is commonly interpreted as someone with a negative and / or anxious attitude – potentially anger. This is also referred to as the *frustration gesture* where the receiver can interpret the message as the person holding back a negative attitude.

The three main positions to hold this gesture are; in front of the face, resting on a desk or in the lap, and (when standing) hands clenched in front of the crotch. Some believe that the higher the person's hands are clenched the more difficult it will be to deal with them, making it important to give them something to hold onto to unlock their fingers – and attitude – although there is no empirical evidence to prove this.

> **Did you know?** Hand-to-mouth gestures are commonly mistaken for a sign of someone telling a lie; however they can also be pacifiers or just a habit of the person talking.

The Steeple

For a long time the steeple gesture has been interpreted as a confidence gesture, or a self assured attitude, and is often seen with superiors giving instructions or advice – as well as body language-trained public figures such as politicians. Sometimes this gesture converts into a prayer-like gesture, which can be interpreted by the receiver as arrogance. Of course - depending on the circumstances and facial expressions - this can also be read as someone being humble, grateful, or even begging for mercy.

The steeple can portray confidence (from the perspective of the sender of the gesture to the receiver of the gesture) – provided it is not overdone, as when over-used this gesture can also come across as arrogance – or as if someone has glued their fingers together.

> **Tip:** It is important to remember that body language has a sender and a receiver – therefore interpretation of gestures can be subjective.

Holding a Hand Behind the Back

Palm-in-Palm
This gesture is common amongst leaders and royalty, as well as policemen, military and people in authority. The emotions attached to this gesture are often confidence and superiority – or wanting to portray confidence – as the person is exposing their vulnerable areas (stomach, heart,

crotch, throat, etc) in an act of fearlessness. Research shows that when someone in a nervous or in a high stress situation can become more confident by adopting this gesture.

Hand-Gripping-Arm

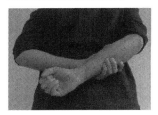

There are several perspectives on this gesture. One is a sign of frustration and self control, with one arm holding the other arm or wrist behind the back, almost as if attempting to prevent the arm from striking out. This interprets that the higher up the arm the holding hand grips, the greater the anger or frustration. It is from this term that, "Get a grip on yourself" originates. These gestures are usually used to disguise nervousness or self restraint, and if you catch yourself doing this, revert back to the Palm-in-Palm behind your back instead.

This gesture can also be interpreted as a subtle self-assurance, so as with most body language interpretations, it will depend on the situation, environment and facial expressions. Also keep in mind that this is a different gesture from the Palm-in-Palm behind the back that looks similar.

Did you know? The palm closed finger pointing gesture can act like a symbolic club, 'beating' listeners into submission.

Thumb Displays

Thumbs usually signify positive emotions, and can be linked to feelings of superiority – indicating self important attitudes. Most "experts" say that thumbs display supremacy, authority and assertiveness, and are usually part of a cluster of other gestures – however it also depends on the baseline of the individual (does the person normally display their thumbs?). Thumb displays are often interpreted as an overall positive gesture.

Thumbs sometimes protrude from the back pockets, where a person may be trying to hide their dominant attitudes. The arms-folded-with-thumbs-point-upwards cluster shows a negative attitude (arms folded – see arm barriers), plus a superior attitude.

Arm Signals

As children we hid behind objects for protection – such as furniture or our mother's dress – when we found ourselves in threatening or undesirable circumstances. As we grew older we developed the habit of folding our arms across our chests to replace solid objects, by placing or holding items in front of us such as a hand bag, brief case or even a coffee cup. The arm barrier unconsciously protects the heart and lung area from injury, protecting oneself from a frontal attack.

Bottom line is, you can often tell if a person has a negative, nervous or defensive attitude by their arms being folded across their chest. Remember to take note however – is it cold? People also do this to keep warm; however there is still some argument that this is displaying a negative attitude towards the cold.

Here are some of the common arm signals for you to become familiar with:

Arms Folded

The arm signal commonly interprets as an attempt to put a barrier between the person (the sender) and something or someone (the receiver) that they are uncomfortable with. This usually occurs anywhere that people may feel insecure, nervous, exposed or uncertain, such as in front of others. Similar to the hand clench, the best way to break an arms fold is to give the person something to hold onto.

The arms folded position can also send the message of being defensive, reserved or closed off, and it is a common arm position for people intentionally portraying intimidation or to make themselves seem bigger (such as security staff and bouncers) to reduce the likelihood of being challenged. It is important to note the facial expressions or emotion (anger, contempt, happy, etc) and the leg positioning (see next chapter) to gain a more accurate interpretation.

Reinforced Arm Folding

Clenched Fist Arm Fold
This arm signal is the same as the arms folded; however the person also has clenched fists. This commonly interprets as a defensive (from the arm folding) *and* aggressive attitude (from the clenched fists). To me this can indicate several possibilities, including frustration and self restraint. Remember to take into account the person's facial expression, leg and body position to gauge a more accurate body language interpretation.

Double Grip Arm Fold
The double grip arm fold is identifiable as the person's hands grip their upper arms, and the most common message this sends is one of self-hugging and self-assuring. Self-hugging gestures tend to occur when people experience negative emotions – such as being nervous – therefore is seen more regularly in places that generate anxiety, such as waiting in a hospital or prior to an exam or driving test.

Tip: For accurate body language reading, read gestures in clusters. Look at everything – not just one gesture – to gain a more accurate story.

Self Hugging / Reassuring

Partial Arm Cross
Similar to the double grip arm fold, this self hugging / reassuring gesture is more commonly seen when a person is facing tense or distressing circumstances. The partial-arm-cross is more favoured with women, and is assumed to recreate the reassurance a hug can provide. I also see this gesture with children who are unsure, such as circumstances like not knowing where to go or who to go to for help. Some people find this comfortable, however remember what messages you could be sending.

Tip: Generally any hand / arm movement that involves holding onto another part of the body can be categorized as a self hugging or reassuring gesture.

The Broken Zipper
The broken zipper self hugging gesture is more commonly seen with men who feel exposed – such as standing in front of a crowd. Someone could be standing in a legs apart crotch display (described in the next chapter) which is a more assertive, confident stance as it shows off the crotch. As a carry on from the animal kingdom, when it comes to crotch displays it tends to indicate one of two things: 1) show it off, or 2) protect from harm. With the exception of wearing clothes, we humans are no different. When we add the broken zipper gesture to the legs apart crotch display, this changes the stance from a "show it off" to "protect from harm". It is assumed that the broken zipper gesture has a man feel more secure as he is protected from a frontal attack.

Cufflink Adjust
Men wearing cufflinks can subtly pose a partial-arm-cross as they fidget with their cufflink (or in the absence of a cufflink, can fidget with a button, a watch, ring, hand, loosen tie, mobile phone, etc), which is speculated to be performed to gain feelings of security, usually seen when crossing in front of a crowd. This could be similar to the table barriers below, where a woman may hold close her purse or handbag for a similar purpose.

Table Barriers

Unsure how your sales meeting, negotiation, or date is going? Offer them a glass of water, coffee or a glass of wine then take note of where they place their cup immediately *after* they take a drink. This will provide you with an indicator of how they feel towards the conversation, sales pitch or date. If they are feeling hesitant, negative or unsure they will likely place their cup between themselves and you to form a single-arm-barrier. However when they are more open they will often place the cup to the side of their body, displaying openness.

This also applies to the positioning of a woman's handbag, or a person's mobile phone or diary, etc.

Did you know? Open palms used to be the symbol to show that no weapons were being concealed.

"It is important to remember that body language has a sender *and* a receiver – therefore interpretation of gestures can be subjective.

Be aware that most body language interpretations and information should be considered anecdotal, unless confirmed by research.

Also, the sender may not intend to portray a particular message; however the receiver may still unconsciously interpret the 'message' incorrectly."
- Stu Dunn

CHAPTER 11
Gestures & Body Language: Legs

"A different suit will get you noticed for a day, but a change of attitude will get you noticed for a life time." - Lao Tsu

Introduction

Legs allow us to walk, run, jump, skip and kick. Perhaps due to legs being positioned furthest from the brain, when it comes to non-verbal communication we tend to be less aware of what our legs are doing. We learn from a very early age to paste on a smile when required, so we become most aware of what our faces are "saying". It could be said that we are virtually oblivious to what our feet are non-verbally portraying. This is why a common body language perspective is that a person's legs and feet are an important source of information about attitudes, and it is difficult to fake gestures in the way we can with our face.

How we walk can potentially tell others a little about what we think of ourselves. Healthy young people tend to walk faster than older people, resulting in their arms swinging higher in front and behind – sometimes appearing as if they are marching. For example, Allan Pease suggests that the exaggerated movement of the military march is to present the interpretation that the marchers are youthful and strong (Pease & Pease, 2009).

The Legs and Lying

Some people tend to increase their lower body movements when they lie; therefore observers have a generally higher chance of spotting a lie if they can see their entire body. This could help to explain why many business people feel more comfortable behind a solid desk as opposed to a glass top table that allows full view of the legs and feet.

> **Tip:** Jiggling the feet can often indicate that the person wants to run away from what is being experienced.

Key Points to Remember

Here are some of the important points to remember from Chapter 10:

- Body language has a sender and a receiver.
- Interpretations can be subjective (particularly out of context using images). Take into account the environment (E.g. the temperature).
- Be aware that people can have their own idiosyncratic habits.
- One gesture can provide an indication towards an interpretation; however try to take into account the face, the body position, arms, hands and legs. Do any other gestures hint towards the same interpretation?

Although this chapter does not cover all possible leg positions, I have broken up the body language of the legs into two categories: Standing Positions and Sitting Positions.

The Four Main Standing Positions

How we stand can say a lot about how we feel, as legs move us towards what we want, and move us away from what we don't want. It is in this way that an individual can reveal where they want to go using their legs and feet, such as wanting to leave a conversation or revealing interest in a person.

Feet Together, At Attention

This standing position can portray neutral intentions, respect or even nervousness depending on the environment and what the rest of the body is saying. It is also common in environments where there is an authority present; such as employees with employers, children with teachers, or the military.

Another place this is seen regularly is the beginning of martial arts forms (also called katas or patterns depending on the martial art). The feet together, hands by sides is generally considered a neutral or starting position, where – depending on the martial art – the hands will normally form fists and raise to the sides before the student moves into the martial arts' stance or begins the form or kata.

Legs Apart, Crotch Display

More common with males than females, this is a standing crotch display. This, along with both feet being evenly weighted, portrays a confident attitude, sending the message that the person is not going anywhere (weight on the feet being evenly distributed) and they are not afraid of attack (open crotch display). From a martial arts / confrontational perspective, this stance demonstrates a balanced position prior to engagement / conflict.

Overall, this standing position is usually an intentional stance that tells the receiver that the person is confident and has no intention of leaving.

The exception to this is where this standing position is accompanied by the hands being in a self hugging or broken zipper position.

Did You Know? Albert Mehrabian is well known for the following statistics: 55% of the messages that we convey to other people are transmitted through body language, 38% is in the tone of voice, and only 7% in the words we use (when verbal context is ambiguous).

These statistics are based on Albert Mehrabian's research from 1967, and have been misquoted and misrepresented regularly, creating two main issues: 1) speakers are led to believe their delivery can make or break their presentation, and 2) encourages presenters to "wing it" and not prepare their presentations.

Although I still use these statistics (mainly for presentations) I do include the caveat; "when verbal context is ambiguous", and warn people about the two main issues as described above.

Foot Forward

The foot forward position generally provides a good indication of the mindset of a person as the majority of the person's body weight shifts to one side to allow the opposite foot to point in the direction where they are focused. In a standing social setting, people tend to point their lead foot towards the most interesting person in the conversation, someone they find the most attractive, or sometimes just the person who is taking their turn talking. It can also indicate when someone wants to escape from a conversation when their lead foot is pointing towards the exit.

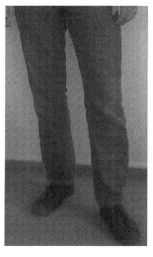

From a defensive perspective, the foot forward position doubles as a ready stance, being prepared for engagement / conflict. The principle remains the same however, as the foot points in the general direction of the target (or stimulus / danger). Most martial arts discourage pointing the toes directly at an opponent as this provides the knee as a target, that if hit straight on, would lock the leg and force the defender down. The direction the front foot faces from the perspective of an opponent can also provide valuable information as to their next move, such as turning the front foot out could indicate a back leg kick, and turning it inwards could indicate a spinning kick. I have found that most experienced martial artists and boxers are already unconsciously aware of people's footwork.

Overall, the foot forward standing position could indicate standing comfortably, showing the leg (such as a modelling pose for photographs) and potentially reveal intentions, attractions and interests.

Leg Cross

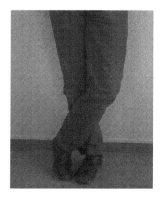

Legs and arms crossed by and large send the message of a closed, submissive, defensive or even angry attitude. The message that the standing leg cross tends to send is one of lacking confidence in the current situation, however this depends on what the rest of the body is saying. For example, the interpretation will differ from the person in the standing leg cross with a self hugging gesture, to the person with more open upper body language. Some researchers have suggested that a common interpretation of a man in the standing leg cross is to protect the crotch, whereas a woman using this stance is indicating she is not open to advances.

Overall, this standing position has many possible interpretations and needs to be read in context. This stance can be depicted as being impatient, insecure and closed off, however under other circumstances it could come off as arrogant, flirty or extremely comfortable (as it is a poor position to defend oneself from). Take in the full picture to allow more understanding of the context.

> **Tip:** Open legs generally sends the message of male confidence whereas closed legs is usually received as a sign of uncertainty.

Sitting Positions

How many hours a day do we spend sitting? First there is breakfast, then sitting in the car in traffic or on the bus or train, followed for many by sitting at a desk all day. Then there is the journey home followed by sitting down to dinner, then in front of the television for the evening. Even excluding any social time this example may be quite an exaggeration, however it is a reality that we tend to sit during a great deal of our lives. People often get restless sitting for too long, and we are inclined to sit in different positions, finding some more comfortable than others.

Below are five examples of common sitting positions. In my opinion, the leg cross and figure four sitting positions do not send a clear message by themselves, as they are extremely common and comfortable sitting positions found around the world. I have however noted additions to these sitting positions that can alter potential interpretations.

<u>Seated Leg Cross</u>

The leg cross has one leg draped over the other (note that this is different from the parallel legs position) and is a very popular sitting position for both men and women. As mentioned above, in my opinion this position does not send a clear message alone. However, when matched with the arms folded this tends to create the message of someone being more defensive, reserved or closed off – particularly if they are also leaning back (of course, being aware of the context / environment – is it cold..?). The leg cross sitting position combined with the hands clenched / interlocked fingers over the knee (sometimes holding the leg) generally sends the frustration message (as with the Chapter 10 gesture) where the receiver can interpret this as holding back a negative attitude, such as anger or nervousness.

Did You Know? Research has shown that people sitting with their arms and legs crossed tend to decline more offers and recall less of conversations and sales pitches than those who sit with their arms and legs in an open position.

Figure Four

The figure four seated position is considered by many body language experts as the seated version of the crotch display, which is perceived as more dominant. I believe that this position does not send a clear message by itself as it is another common comfortable seated position (although it is worth mentioning that in certain parts of the world – mainly Asia and the Middle East – it is considered insulting to display the soles of your shoes, therefore this position will not be as common in those areas of the world).

Interpretations change quickly, however, when for example folding the arms (as above) can send the message of being defensive or closed off. Grasping the top leg makes the figure four leg clamp which can portray a competitive or conflicting attitude or be seen as a self-assuring or self-hugging gesture. Leaning back in the figure four seated position with the hands behind the head generally sends the message of arrogance.

Overall with seated leg cross and figure four positions, look for information from other sources such as the face, body position, hands and arms, to piece together a more accurate interpretation.

Tip: In a sales situation, asking for the sale when the customer is sitting back with their legs crossed and arms folded is not the best time as they are demonstrating strong evidence of someone being closed off to the sale. Find a way for them to lean forward and uncross their arms and legs, such as showing them a brochure on the desk in front of them – once they have broken the negative position the chances are they will be more open to the sale. Studies have also indicated that most people make their final decisions when both feet are on the ground.

Ankle Lock

The female version of the ankle lock normally has the knees held together with the feet off to one side, whereas the male version has the knees out and is generally interpreted as a less dominant seated crotch display.

A common interpretation of the ankle lock is someone holding back a negative emotion – however – some people also "just find this comfortable" for the same reasons as arm folding. It is worth noting that an arrogant person may outstretch their legs crossed at the ankle, and as they become less sure of themselves (such as during a police interview) their feet gradually pull back under the chair indicating that the arrogance has been replaced with unease, nervousness, or another negative emotion or attitude.

Tips: When someone feels defensive or insecure, it's likely that crossed arms and legs will feel more comfortable, as it matches their emotional state.

Parallel Legs

The parallel legs seated position is considered to have two main purposes; 1) it is a comfortable sitting position for most women due to the arrangement of leg and hip bones, and 2) to draw attention to the legs.

Hopefully after you have read this far you will now consider that this position is merely a comfortable sitting position and also means very little by itself. Add folded arms and it could be interpreted as impatience (particularly if the top leg is jiggling – a common indication that a woman may be irritated and want to leave the situation). Add the hand clasp over the knee and it could be seen as a self-hugging gesture. Add sitting on the hands and this could provide insight to a non-verbal "biting of one's tongue" or self-restraint.

The Legs Help Tell the Story

If a lot of the body language of the legs is so subjective, why have I included this chapter? The first reason is that I am hoping to shine some light on some of the body language myths (such as sitting in a figure four means you are confident). Hopefully you will see that everything depends on taking in the whole story, which is my second reason for including this chapter; looking at the face, body position (which way the body is facing), the hands, arms and legs creates a more complete story – with the final piece in the puzzle being the context of the body language. What has happened leading up to the moment you are analysing? What else is going on? What else is in the environment? Are there any extraneous variables that could explain the body language or alter a person's posture (such as cold weather to explain arms folded or hunching, a loud noise to explain a neck turtling or wince etc).

CHAPTER 12
Gestures & Body Language: Emblems, Speech Illustrators & Manipulators

"Gestures are - more often than not - hand, head and face movements. Their usual interpretation is to illustrate speech, convey verbal meanings, and to lighten the cognitive load while searching for the correct thing to say to ensure more rapid communication" - David Matsumoto (2012)

Introduction

After becoming familiar with the common hand, arm and leg gestures, it is time to introduce emblems, speech illustrators and manipulators (sometimes referred to as pacifiers), which will lead us nicely into Part 3: Detection Deception – The Science of Evaluating Truthfulness and Credibility. Considered by some as the holy grail of non-verbal deception leakage, these gestures will complete our introduction to gestures and body language, and in my opinion, be the only body language resource you will need for interpreting the messages others are non-verbally receiving. With one major exception: cultures. Facial expressions are universal, as are body language interpretations. What are not universal are cultural gestures, signs, emblems, etc – I will briefly mention several examples, however exploring cultural gestures is outside of the scope of this book.

The Origins of the Thumbs Up

Peter Quennell – author of the 1971 book *The Colosseum A History of Rome from the Time of Nero* – suggests the origins of the "thumbs up" gesture is said to have come from the Roman gladiatorial times to indicate whether a gladiator will live or die – however there is contradicting evidence as to whether the thumb up meant to spare the fighter or not. Even today the interpretation of the thumbs up gesture is different depending on where in the world you live. It would seem at first glance that much of the western world has adopted the meaning of this symbol to mean "good", "ok" or "yes" – generally some kind of positive meaning – as well as being used for hitchhiking (the hitchhiking thumb). However this can also mean the number one, used to indicate directions, or indicate an insult of a sexual nature.

Cultural Differences with Gestures

Another example of a cultural difference with gestures is the a-ok symbol, where the thumb and forefinger touch to make a circle can mean just that – everything is a-ok. In some Mediterranean countries such as Turkey, this gesture is an insult better described as a-hole or accusing someone of being homosexual, and in certain parts of Europe the a-ok symbol is an insult suggesting "you are nothing", "zero" or "worthless". In sign language this is the symbol for the number 9, or placing ones nose through the "O" in many continental European countries means "drunk".

Tip: I want to emphasis that there is a very real danger of misinterpreting someone's body language, due to not baselining properly (finding out what someone's normal behaviour is before making an interpretation). It is missing this step where innocent people's idiosyncratic habits and cultural differences (where they are in a culture that does not recognise the behaviour) can be mistaken as deceptive.

Ekman and Friesen's 1974 Nursing Experiment

In 1974 Ekman & Friesen designed one of psychology's first non-verbal communication deception experiments where ER nurses were asked to watch positive (such as a happy or uplifting scene) or negative (such as live amputations and burn victims receiving treatment) film clips, and describe one of the gruesome scenes as pleasant to an interviewer. The nurses were filmed, and their films were shown to a large range of professionals. After observing baseline footage of the nurse's normal behaviour, the results indicated that when the viewer saw just the face of the nurse, the untrained lie detector had a very low chance of correctly picking deception (50 / 50). On the other hand, the same untrained lie detectors became much more accurate (around 50% - 65%) when they were able to see the body language of the nurses.

This suggests that no matter how good someone is at reading faces, being able to see the body will increase your chances of detection. With the body, the non-verbal leakage acts like a gestural "slip-of-the-tongue".

Did you know? The handshake evolved as a way of men agreeing to a deal and showing each other that no weapons were concealed in their sleeves, as was common with the Romans.

The Difference Between Emblems and Speech Illustrators

Trying to remember the differences between emblems and speech illustrators can be challenging as they are often confused with each other, so I have included two helpful points:

1) Is the gesture done with words? It is a speech illustrator.
2) Is the gesture done without words? It is an emblem.

"He that has eyes to see and ears to hear may convince himself that no mortal can keep a secret. If his lips are silent, he chatters with his fingertips; betrayal oozes out of him at every pore." - Sigmund Freud

Emblems

An emblem is a gesture that can replace words, and have very precise meanings which is known to everyone within their culture group e.g. a shrug would normally mean; "I don't know", "I'm helpless", "What does it matter?". Wrist shrugs (a small rotation of the hands) and mouth shrugs (normally depicted by FACS codes 15+17, the lower lip depressor and the raising of the chin boss) also carry the emblemic same message.

Emblems are done mostly on purpose; however they can also act very much like a slip in body movement – or a non-verbal slip-of-the-tongue. When someone is trying to conceal information or how they feel, they will often only perform a fragment of the emblem, not the entire action. Most emblems are performed in front of a person, waist to neck height.

Common Emblem Gestures

With there being so many emblems – with even more cultural variations – the following list is only a starting guide to assist with your understanding:

Head nod.   The emblemic meaning of the nod in most cultures is yes (with the side to side head wobble in India and Sri Lanka also meaning yes).

Head shake.   In most cultures, this means no. Charles Darwin (1913) suggested that babies search for their mother's milk by moving their head up and down (like the head nod) and decline milk by turning their head from side to side (like the head shake).

Fist clench.	The fist clench generally signifies anger or frustration (which is part of anger), where the fists are ready to strike.
Pointing.	Pointing using the forefinger means something like "over there" or "that way". When waved up and down the meaning shifts to a scolding or "I'm warning you". When the forefinger sways from side to side the emblemic message is one of a warning or "tsk tsk". When used to emphasis words (as a speech illustrator), body language experts believe the message is one of a symbolic club, attempting to non-verbally "bash" listeners into submission. Placing one index finger on top of the other and sliding it down the finger normally means "shame on you".

Turning the hand palm-up with the forefinger out and curl it back towards the body creates the "come here" beckoning gesture. |
Hand behind ear.	The hand behind the ear gesture indicates that someone can not hear what was being said, and can indicate to the recipient to speak louder or to increase the volume.
Waving.	Depending on the context, this normally means "hello" or "goodbye". It can also mean "over here", and when done with both hands can mean "watch out".
Thumbs up.	As previously mentioned, this could mean "good", "number one" or "up yours".
A-ok.	Again, this has many different meanings, including "all good", "zero", "worthless" or "a-hole".
Peace / Victory.	The two fingers up with fingers forward can mean "peace", "victory" or "two", and when moving the tops of these fingers up and down changes the meaning to imitate rabbit ears or to make a non-verbal speech mark. Turn the hand

around so the back of the hand is facing outwards with the two fingers raised can also mean "two", however this is also an "f-you" insult.

Shrug.

A double shoulder shrug tends to mean "I don't know" amongst other ideas previously mentioned, where wrist (a small rotation of the hands, suggests that nothing in concealed) and mouth shrugs (normally depicted by FACS codes 15+17, the lower lip depressor and the raising of the chin boss) also carry the emblemic same message. Single shoulder shrugs tends to indicate less confidence in what the person is saying which can be quite telling with detecting deception – not that a lie has definitely been told, rather that further questioning should be made around the specific topic where the single shrug occurred.

Did You Know? The "two finger salute" – also known as "The Longbowman Salute" – originated during the Hundred Year War around 1415. According to historians, whenever the French captured the English and Welsh longbowmen, they would cut off their "bow fingers" so they could no longer use a longbow. The two finger salute became a gesture indicating that the English and Welsh still had their bow fingers.

"The most important thing in communication is hearing what isn't said." - Peter F. Drucker

The "f-you" finger gestures are actually very common if you look for them, from someone choosing to use their middle finger to push their glasses back up their nose, to resting their chin on their two fingers in a subtle two-finger salute.

As you can see in the picture to the left, Christchurch New Zealand Police Dog Handler Bruce Lamb displayed his feelings during a television interview about the sentencing of Christopher Smith, the man who had shot him as well as shot and killed his police dog 18 months prior.

Emblems and Detecting Deceit

Emblems can commonly used to detect deception, for example when someone saying "Yes" while actually shaking their head "No" at the same time. A single shoulder shrug tends to indicate less confidence in what the person is saying, clenched fists could indicate anger or self restrain. The lip press is another indictor of anger or self restraint, some suggesting it is symbolic of keeping ones mouth shut to avoid saying something that could be detrimental to their cause.

Not all liars will make an emblemic slip. When emblems are not performed intentionally, they can be interpreted in a similar way as the slip of the tongue, leaking information the person is potentially trying to conceal, and generally emblems increase rather than decrease in deceit.

"What you do speaks so loud that I cannot hear what you say."
- Ralph Waldo Emerson

Speech Illustrators

Speech illustrators "illustrate" speech as it is spoken, and are part of our normal everyday body language and gesturing that help us to describe something in particular. Speech illustrators often help to lighten the cognitive load, and are used to explain ideas that are difficult to put into words, when a person can't find a word, or to give directions, for example. The more attached, involved or emotional someone is with what is being said (such as being excited, distressed or angry) generally increases the amount of speech illustrators being performed.

Speech illustrators are part of our everyday body language, but an absence of them can have someone look "stiff" or uncomfortable.

Types of Speech Illustrators

According to Efron (1941) & Freedman & Hoffmann (1967) (as cited by Matsumoto & Hwang, 2012) there are several categories of speech illustrators, each having their own uses during speech:

- <u>Batons</u> are movements that emphasise a word or phrase (such as an orchestra conductor or a politician who raises and drops their hand as they make points). These do not tend to have any meaning without the accompanying words.
- <u>Pictographs</u>, which draw a picture of what is being referred to (such as indicating the size and shape of a fish or depicting a shape by drawing it in the air).
- <u>Deictic movements</u> are visual pointing aids (such as pointing up a street while giving directions, or pointing at an object while saying "that one").
- <u>Spatial movements</u> illustrate spatial relationships (such as indicating the relative distance between two landmarks using the hands).
- <u>Kinetographs</u>, which depict bodily action (such as hitting, throwing, ducking, etc).

It is usually the hands that illustrate speech, although head (indicating a direction), as well as the brow, upper eyelids and the entire upper body can also work. Speech illustrators are often required for successful public speaking, although it is worth mentioning that certain cultures illustrate much more than others.

> **Tip:** A common speech illustrator is describing "how big the fish was" – try doing this without using your hands. The conversation would change to something like; "The fish was approximately 30 cm long by about 10 cm high..." We can also use speech illustrators while on the phone to a certain extent. Even though the other person can't see us, illustrating can help with the mental processes of retelling the story.

<u>Illustrators and Detecting Deceit</u>

When it comes to clues to detecting deception, it is necessary to note a *decrease* in the number of illustrators shown – in other words – when a person illustrates less than usual. This requires benchmarking / obtaining a baseline for the person, becoming aware of what their "normal" is, to be able to appreciate what may be considered "abnormal". A word of warning; someone talking cautiously during speech does not always have to do with deceit, which is why it is important to benchmark behaviour.

During their in-depth studies of many different methods of detecting deception through behavioural cues, Porter & ten Brinke (2010) validated illustrators (either an increase or decrease depending on the person's baseline), an increase in speech pauses, and blink rates (again, either an increase or decrease from baseline) as being the most reliable indicators of deception when compared to baseline responses.

> **Tip:** If a person illustrates *less* than their usual, it could be cause for further questioning. Although it is more common for someone to lessen their speech illustrators while lying, I have meet individuals who did the exact opposite – which is again why baselining is extremely important.

The Reduction of Speech Illustrators

If a fairly reliable indicator of deception is the reduction of speech illustrators, it is helpful to know what might cause this to happen to avoid jumping to conclusions:

- The person may have a complete lack of emotional investment in what they are saying; they could feel bored, disinterested or even depressed. For example of this could be someone who has been interviewed on the same subject over and over again and is no longer emotionally invested. A depressed individual not only illustrates less, they also have less movement in the upper parts of their face (see Chapter 6). This reason for the reduction of speech illustrators is not caused by deception.

- The other main reason for the reduction of speech illustrators is when a person is having trouble deciding exactly what to say, weighing each word carefully, and considering what to say before speaking. This can also happen during an unrehearsed presentation as it takes a lot of effort to recall what to say, however this can also occur when a liar invents a story.

> **SDL Interview Analysis**
> In 2011, I analysed the police interview of a teenage girl who was being questioned in relation to the arson of a portable toilet. Throughout most of the interview she kept her arms folded, only occasionally unfolding them to nervously fidget (see manipulators in the next section) or to use speech illustrators to help her describe directions, the order of events, and the setting of the fire. As she was blaming someone else for starting the fire, her right hand absently imitated the motions of using a lighter, and throughout the video I gathered enough evidence to believe that the girl was in fact the culprit who started the fires.
>
> Her imitating starting the fire may have been an emblemic slip (where she accidentally let on that she had done this); however this is not strongly supported as it only happened one time throughout

the interview. What I noticed was that the girl only used speech illustrators when she was telling the truth overall, such as describing the correct directions, putting the order of events into the right order, and how the fire was started. Her illustrators stopped as soon as she blamed someone else for starting the fires (i.e. as soon as she started to lie again) as she had been the one to start it.

The clue to deceit comes from noting a decrease in the number of illustrators shown overall – or at least doing so less than usual. It is essential to have an idea of the person's baseline to what their usual behaviour and illustrating is.

Manipulators

Manipulators (also referred to as pacifiers) include all movements where one part of the body manipulates another part of the body, such as; massaging (an arm, hand or neck), rubbing (the neck, hands together or legs), holding (anything that creates a self-hugging gesture), picking (could be nails or teeth, or in some instances it could be picking lint from a coat) or scratching (any body part). In most cases, manipulators increase with discomfort, anxiety and stress. These are however unreliable cues to deceit by themselves, therefore should be noted when found amongst a cluster of other cues.

Tip: In most cases, manipulators increase with discomfort. However, manipulators also increase when someone is very comfortable (such as at home watching the television). This is when all manner of manipulator behaviour can occur, from nail biting to ear picking. With this in mind, remember to be aware of the context and environment.

Typically the hand is the manipulator, and the common body parts to fidget with being the hair, ears, nose, teeth or crotch. The tongue is a common manipulator against the cheeks and with the teeth, and biting or licking the lips is another. Manipulators can also range from a leg rubbing another leg to fidgeting with nearby objects such as car keys, pens, or an empty mug. Manipulators that involve picking, are common with people who feel shame (Ekman, 2009).

Manipulators and Detecting Deceit

Manipulators can be quite unreliable by themselves as signs of deceit because:

- People are so different, therefore vary a great deal in how many manipulators and what kinds of manipulators they may or may not display.
- The Othello error (showing signs of fear at NOT being believed) also alters the interpretation of manipulators as a deception clue, as manipulators, increase when people are uncomfortable, distressed or anxious about anything. I will go more in depth with errors and precautions in the next part of the book.
- An educated liar can attempt to hide or resist showing manipulators if they believe that displaying them may indicate deception.

PART 2 – WHAT ARE THESE IMAGES SAYING?

Review Part 1 *and* 2. Write down what you think these images are saying. Look at the facial expressions, hands, arm positions, the body language of the legs and any gestures for the people in each image. Suggested answers can be found in the Appendix at the back of the book

Image 7

Image 9

PART 3

DETECTING DECEPTION – THE SCIENCE OF EVALUATING TRUTHFULNESS AND CREDIBILITY –

CHAPTER 13
Speech and Deception

"People will believe a big lie sooner than a little one. And if you repeat it frequently enough, people will sooner than later believe it." - Walter Langer

Introduction

The word communication comes from the Latin word *commūnicāre* (which means 'to share"), and can share messages both verbally and non-verbally. In previous chapters I have only covered the first two non-verbal channels of communication; the face and gestures and body language. The purpose of the previous chapters has been to prepare you for reading and understanding micro expressions and body language, and becoming aware of clues to deception. This chapter introduces how a deceitful person's voice, verbal style and verbal statements can betray their lie, give you an opportunity to test yourself as you go, as well as providing an introduction to discourse analysis and the Scientific Content Analysis.

There is no single sign of deception. There is no one gesture, facial expression or muscle twitch that means someone is being deceitful; there are only clues that the person is poorly prepared, and shows clues of emotions that do not fit the person's line or intent. The liar's words normally gain the most attention from the target, however these are the easiest to falsify. After the words, the next cue to gain the attention of the target (interviewer, or person being lied to) is the subject's (or liar's) displayed emotions. Dr. Paul Ekman says; "The face is directly connected to those areas of the brain involved in emotion, and words are not." Similar to expressions, the voice is tied to areas of the brain involved in emotion. Although the body is an excellent source of leakage and deceptive clues, it is not directly linked to the areas of the brain involving emotions. This makes concealing a body movement easier than concealing facial expressions or emotion related voice changes, however targets (the person being lied to) can often ignore body movements while concentrating on other areas for leakage. And when a liar is concentrating on keeping facial expressions and voice in check – the body language tends to be forgotten, which results in slips.

These slips are what provide us with information on deception leakage, hotspots, or clues to deception.

How Many Ways Can You Say?

Let us have another look at Albert Mehrabian's findings (as mentioned in Chapter 11, these results are not based on everyday life) that 55% of the messages that we convey to other people are transmitted through body language, 38% is in the tone of voice, and only 7% in the words we use (when verbal context is ambiguous). Part 1 and 2 of this book covered a large amount of information that would sit in the 55% category, which leaves 38% for the tone of voice, and only 7% for what is actually being said.

You have likely heard the term; "It's not what you say, but how you say it." This means that we are already aware that there are non-verbal elements to the spoken word and voice, and they are just as important as what is actually being said. For example, how many ways can you say the phrase: "That was really nice"? We could emphasis the word "was", suggesting that what we were talking about is potentially no longer nice or has occurred in the past. Emphasising the word "that" could indicate surprise at it being nice. We could say the whole phrase with sincerity, indicating that whatever we were talking about we really did like, or we could say the phrase in a sarcastic tone, which again, changes the meaning. Shouting "that was really nice" has a different meaning from saying "that was really nice" with tears in our eyes. Every conceivable way of saying this phrase changes the message being sent.

> **Tip:** In my opinion, couples become very wise to each other's tones and how words are said. Saying something as simple as; "I'll help" could backfire if spoken with a sigh, the tone was harder than normal or if it was said in a condescending or sarcastic manner, for example. This is also how some couples can pick up on "something not being right" with their partner – as well as many ways that arguments can start.
>
> Whether we know it or not, we're already quite sensitive to the non-verbal aspect of the spoken word.

"One should always look for a possible alternative, and provide against it. It is the first rule of criminal investigation." –
Sherlock Holmes

Voice

The voice refers to everything involved in speech other than the words themselves. The issue here is that most of the deceptive indicators are subjective, what sounds stressed to one person may not be to another, with tempos, tone and volume changes sometimes being quite difficult to notice.

Pauses

The most common vocal deception clues are **pauses, being too long or too frequent**. Suspicion is aroused when a person hesitates when starting to speak (particularly if the start is answering a question). Too many shorter pauses may also cause suspicion. In the exercises, pauses will be indicated with three full stops that look like this ...

> **Tip:** The most common vocal deception clues are pauses, being too long or too frequent.

Speech Errors

Speech errors may also be a deception clue, including **repetitions** and **partial words** (similar to stuttering). In the exercises, speech errors will be inferred with a hyphen, such as "T-to be clear".

Speech Dis-fluencies

These account for the **seemingly random and meaningless sounds, sighs, and pauses that fill our normal everyday speech**. When people are confident about what they are saying, their statements are straightforward, such as;

"I came home last night around eleven thirty",
"She can be hard to work with, but we get along okay",
"What is it you want to know?"

Stressed or nervous subjects often try to slow their speech to gain more time to think. As silence makes most people uncomfortable, subjects feel the need to fill the pauses with sound. In the exercises, speech dis-fluencies will be inferred as they are in the examples below:

"**Uh**, I came home last night around eleven thirty",
"She can be, **like**, hard to work with *sigh* but we get along okay",
Speaker clears their throat "What is it you want to know?"

The Sound of the Voice

The sound of the voice often describes what emotion a person feels. The most documented vocal sign of emotion is pitch, which becomes higher with anger, fear or excitement, and drops with sadness. Louder faster speech is associated with anger and fear, with softer slower speech with sadness. These changes in the voice are produced by emotion and are not easy to conceal. Equally, no pitch change or emotion can be cause for alarm. Detection apprehension will produce the sound of fear in someone's voice. Deception guilt often sounds like sadness (Ekman, 2009).

Voice Exercises

List any pauses, speech errors and / or speech dis-fluencies that you identify from the list below. Answers can be found at the back of the book.

"Where was I? *um* I was going for a walk then,"
E.g. Where was I? could be repetition, and *um* a speech error.

1) "I…think…it looks great,"

2) "I d-don't *um* …know *cough*, …maybe, maybe one of the other kids took it?"

3) "…I-I went to the store about 10 *um*, yeah, about 10,"

4) "What year did I graduate? I graduated in 2005,"

5) "Tell you a time when I…well…*um*…I – when I was there *um*. What did you want to know exactly?"

6) "What time? Think it was 8 – no – 9 o'clock,"

7) "I have…never…we don't hit our *clear throat* kids. They're good kids,"

Verbal Style

Carelessness, slips of the tongue (or Freudian slips), forgetting familiar names and details of which should, under normal circumstances, be easy to recall, evasiveness of answering questions and deflection are all clues that there may be an internal conflict.

Slips of the Tongue

Also referred to as Freudian slips, a slip of the tongue is a mistake in speech that often betrays an unconscious thought or feeling. They do not prove deception or the intent to deceive, however they are often revealing. Interviewed parents who know what happened to their missing children occasionally make the mistake of changing tense; "She **was** an amazing child" rather than "She *is* an amazing child". This slip of the tongue reveals that the interviewed parent either knew (or strong suspected) their child was already dead.

Slip of the Tongue Catches a Killer and Accomplice

On 4 August 2002, school caretaker Ian Huntley murdered two 10-year-old girls in a small village in Cambridgeshire. Maxine Carr was interviewed and accidentally slipped into the past tense twice while speaking about the missing girls. This lead to further questioning and investigation, and the remainder of the girls' burnt clothes in Huntley's possession. Carr's slip of the tongue indicated that she knew more about the disappearance than she was letting on.

Non-Contracted Denials

"I **did not** do it!" is a non-contracted denial, compared to a contracted denial; "I **didn't** do it!" Guilty people will often emphasize the "*not*", using more formal grammar than usual. Non-contracted denials are usually spoken slowly, purposefully, perhaps reflecting more consideration and less emotion than a genuine plea of innocence – perhaps also trying to oversell their honesty.

Tip: Guilty people will often emphatically emphasize the "not", using more formal grammar than they would usually. However, some truthful people do this too – so remember to baseline! Also remember that just one indicator of deceit does not equal deceit; look for hot spots and clusters – more on this over the next few chapters.

Specific Denials

People who are telling the truth tend to offer grand denials of any offense, such as; "I'm not seeing anyone else." Liars on the other hand are more likely to make their denials much more specific, such as; "I'm not seeing [*this particular person*]". As the denial has been made more specific, the person considers it is no longer a lie.

Pronoun Inaccuracies / Inconsistencies

Pronouns (I, you, me for example) that make a statement personal, as with distancing statements (covered in the next section), are often absent in a liar's statement. For example; "Got up. Had a shower and changed, then arrived at work." Another way someone might distance themselves through language while answering questions they find threatening is by replacing the pronoun "I" with "you". For example; "You just don't do that kind of thing," or "You would not want to walk there at night."

Anger Management Group

During a workshop one time I was asked by a participant why men in his anger management group very rarely used the word "I", and mainly used "you" in their sharing. In my opinion, this is most likely to be a way for these men to subconsciously distance themselves from – not only the situation and circumstances that led them sitting in an anger management group – but also distancing themselves from having to take personal responsibility for their own anger and actions.

It is for this reason I've included a discourse analysis exercise on the topic.

Verbal Style Exercises

List any slips of the tongue, non-contracted denials, specific denials and pronoun inaccuracies. Answers can be found at the back of the book in the Appendix.

"Where was I Friday? I <u>do not</u> remember, <u>I am not</u> someone that keeps track of time,"
E.g. <u>do not</u> and <u>I am not</u> are non-contracted denials

1) "We need laws that protect everyone. Men and women, straights and gays, regardless of sexual perversion…ah, persuasion…"

2) *Question:* "Are we negotiating with any other media company?"
Answer: "We have not been negotiating with Mayfair Media,"

3) "I was not able to identify the perpetrator before they knocked me out and took Gail. Gail meant everything, please find them,"

4) "It happened around 1 o'clock? I wasn't even home by then, I got home about 2:30,"

5) "People who do these sorts of things... you just don't do that sort of thing,"

"Perhaps, when a man has special knowledge and special powers like my own, it rather encourages him to seek a complex explanation when a simpler one is at hand."
- Sherlock Holmes

Verbal Statements

Distancing language is common with an individual who is attempting to create a distance between themselves and their guilt, or the lie in question (such as using language to describe someone as "that woman" or "she" instead of using their name). Reliable clues to deceit and contradictions are common with an individual who fabricates information and shows an increased vagueness.

Repeated Questions (or Parrot Statements)

If someone **repeats your question back to you in full** they may be trying to buy some time to consider how to answer the question. Partial repeats are quite normal and often used to gain clarification of a question; however a repeat of the entire question can indicate they don't want to answer it or have not yet come up with an answer. In a job interview "tell me a time when you demonstrated" question, it is expected that some people may not answer immediately as they have to recall a time. It does become more suspicious however if the circumstances and answer of the question should be easily accessible, such as; "Who were you with three hours ago at the Mall?"

Guilt Statements

These are used as **an attempt to put the target (interviewer) onto the defence** in a deliberate attempt to divert the line of questioning because the interviewer must now defend themselves or get caught up in an off-topic. An example of this could be; "I've served on the school council for five years – I've done nothing but good things for the school. Tell me, what have *you* done?"

Too Little or Too Much Statements

A truthful person answering a question may leave out minor details or add a few irrelevant ones, however overall the question will be answered. A deceitful response tends **to omit major details that they think could be incriminating, or they may provide an unnecessarily lengthy and wordy answer**. This tactic is used by politicians when trying to avoid answering a specific question (to avoid being forced to lie or incriminate themselves). Notice if the person answering the question uses a lot of words while not answering the question?

Deflection Statements

These responses **ignore or deflect your question**, often throwing one back at you. This is commonly achieved with answering one question by asking another.

Protest Statements

These statements are used to **remind the interviewer that nothing about their past indicates they are untrustworthy**. Building on the example from the guilt statement, "How dare you ask me that? I'm a good person, go to church, have three kids at this school and have served on the school council for five years – I've done nothing but good things for the school. Tell me, what have *you* done?" This is an example of how a protest and guilt statement can easily throw the interviewer off the topic of inquiry and into self-defence.

Reinforcing Statements

Also referred to as bolstering or strengthening statements, these are when **liars add phrases to their statements to come across as convincingly and sincerely as possible**. For example, when stating; "To be honest", "To tell you the truth", "As far as I recall", "You'll never believe this, but..." and "I swear to God / honest to God".

Distancing Statements

It is not uncommon for liars to unconsciously **avoid referring to themselves in their lies, and thus distancing themselves (and personal pronouns) from the lie through their statement**. For example; "This would be a great thing for you to buy" rather than "I think this would be a great thing for you to buy". Distancing statements also tend to impersonalise others (such as; "that woman") and uses minimalising language (such as; "He did ok").

Bill Clinton's Public Denial of Sexual Relations

This is Bill Clinton's public denial, word for word:

"I want to say one thing to the American people. I want you to listen to me. I'm going to say this again: I did not have sexual relations with that woman, Miss Lewinsky. I never told anybody to lie, not a single time; never. These allegations are false. And I need to go back to work for the American people. Thank you" - *Bill Clinton.*

If you have the opportunity I would recommend looking this up on You Tube, just so you can fully absorb just how many clues to deception Mr. Clinton is leaking. Very briefly, his body language during this statement is the use of the finger-club baton (to hammer his point across – not related to deception), while he makes a non-contracted denial (did not), and distancing statement (that woman) – which makes a small cluster of clues for deception.

Euphemisms

Euphemisms are mild or indirect ways of toning down something that could be incriminating, unpleasant or embarrassing, and is a form of distancing language, intentionally dulling down the words used. For example; "Why did you steal that?" could be responded with "I did not take anything". This lacks emotion, and replaced "steal" with a much gentler "take". Other examples are replacing assault with "push" or "argument" with the word "discussion".

Putting the Voice, Verbal Style & Statements Together Exercises

Label the following combining everything you have learnt so far in this chapter, from the voice, verbal style and verbal statements.

1) "Where was I Thursday night at 7 o'clock? I... I don't recall..., I- as I don't wear a watch it's hard to say. I t-think I was *clears throat*, yes, I was driving home,"

2) "I do not know what you are talking about; I do not frequent those kinds of places,"

3) "To be honest, I love what you have done with the place. And frankly, I do not know what the critics were talking about,"

4) "Did I punch him? *cough* No, I did not push him. I'm someone that keeps his cool,"

5) "I got up, made breakfast, had a shower, then headed off to work about 7:30. The traffic was bad, so got to work about 8:45. When I got home the place had been trashed, including my stamp collection, which was insured separately,"

6) "I have people who do that sort of thing for me, why would I need to go there?"

7) "Fight? Yes, we had a disagreement that night, *um* b-but you've got to understand… that woman is difficult sometimes. It was not my fault – I mean that she left upset that night. My wife has done it before, so I was not worried,"

8) "How dare you! You're the last person who can point fingers! Don't you remember the last time *you* made a mistake – you have no right accusing me of anything like this – have I ever done this before?"

Watch *and* Listen for Clusters

Using the clusters of verbal cues against the subject's non-verbal behaviour is an extremely effective formula in detecting deception, with studies having revealed that solely listening to what is said and how it is said can increase the chance of detecting deception.

Additional Note

Machines such as voice stress analysers detect stress – not lying. There is no specific "voice sign" of deceit, only negative emotions. This creates dangers where liars can be missed who do not demonstrate negative emotions, and also incriminate the innocent who are upset. In my opinion voice stress analysers could be used as shortcuts for finding specific areas in an interview where the subject's voice pitch may have changed (indicating an emotion / stress), which can then allow a more thorough analysis on the face, body, and words to take place.

Introduction to Discourse Analysis

Discourse analysis is an area of linguistics that looks at how people construct a version of the world using language – along with other forms of communication. For example, the freedom fighter versus the terrorist; each has different perspectives on the world, reflected by different terms.

As Arthur Conan Doyle's character Sherlock Holmes suggests; "Data! Data! Data! I can't make bricks without clay." As a potter requires clay to mold, a builder needs materials with which to build, and social psychologists require data to work with. Looking from the social constructionism perspective, there is however, a rich amount of social psychological data right under everyone's noses - quite literally - the language that comes out of our mouths, and discourse analysis. "…it is the language they [participants] speak that is the site of investigation," (Widdicombe, 1993, p. 109). The key form of exercising this critical social psychology is through discourse analysis, as this fully enables the educated analyst to understand our social world through language, the raw data of talk and text (Tuffin, 2005). "Reality is in some part created by the manner in which an account is put together," (Tuffin, 2005, p. 92). Discourse analysis follows the assumption that language is action orientated (it does things), and implicated how, through social outcomes, the construction, function and variability of how an account has been assembled.

Beginning Analysis

Below is data from a recorded interview that took place on a street in London. The speaker is a male punk who talks about the events leading up to a riot which occurred following a concert (Widdicome & Wooffitt, 1990, 1995) with reference of interpretation from Tuffin (2005).

1   And the police were all outside there at the concert
2   There wasn't a bit of trouble,
3   apart from say one or two wee scraps, you know.
4   But that happens…every gig there's a scrap –
5   There's always somebody that doesn't like somebody else.
6   It doesn't matter what it is, it's always happening,

7   you know that you cannot stop that.
8   And we go outside and there they are –
9   Fucking eight hundred Old Bill,
10   just waiting for the chance –
11   riot shields, truncheons, and you're not doing nothing –
12   you're only trying to get down to the tube and go home.
13   So what do they do? You're walking by
14   and they're pushing you with their truncheons
15   and they start hitting the odd punk here and there.
16   And what happens?
17   The punks rebel – they don't like getting hit
18   in the face with a truncheon, nobody does.
19   So what do you do?
20   You push the copper back and what happens?
21   Ten or twelve of them are beating
22   the pure hell out of some poor bastard
23   who's only trying to keep somebody off his back.
24   Now that started a riot.

Culturally specific words: gig (concert), wee (small) truncheon (baton), copper (police), Old Bill (police), tube (underground rail).

First, read to get an idea of the overall text and follow the basic plot.

<u>The Police</u>

1   And the police were all outside there at the concert
8   And we go outside and there they are –
9   Fucking eight hundred Old Bill,
10   just waiting for the chance –
11   riot shields, truncheons, and you're not doing nothing –

Creates a sense of threat. Increasing the size of the police presence (800) helps to increase the threat. We are not interested in this analysis as to whether it was true, only that the speaker felt the need to describe it as such.

Line 10 suggests that the police are far from passive, perhaps even hungry for a confrontation, with line 11 reinforcing this further.

13   So what do they do? You're walking by
14   and they're pushing you with their truncheons
15   and they start hitting the odd punk here and there.

Rhetorical question, setting the stage to continue story. Line 14 the "pushing" appears unprovoked, in contrast to line 13's "walking by".

17 The punks rebel – they don't like getting hit
18 in the face with a truncheon, nobody does.

Contributes to the overall construction of police violence and aggression.

20 You push the copper back and what happens?
21 Ten or twelve of them are beating
22 the pure hell out of some poor bastard

The police receive a "push" from a punk which then describes an apparent over reaction and provides a ratio of 10-12:1. The single punk is portrayed as a victim received a beating, which acts to further invoke sympathy to the speaker.

The Punks

2   There wasn't a bit of trouble,
3   apart from say one or two wee scraps, you know.
4   But that happens…every gig there's a scrap –
5   There's always somebody that doesn't like somebody else.
6   It doesn't matter what it is, it's always happening,
7   you know that you cannot stop that.
8   And we go outside and there they are –

Line 2 introduces trouble, however line 3 creates an exception. Denial of trouble could make the speaker untrustworthy, therefore there is an admission. "Scraps" is used as a euphemism to tone down the fights or punch ups, perhaps even having them appear as friendly play fights. "Wee" further downplays this.

Line 4 – the speaker talks as if this is quite normal (always / every), and used to strongly persuade listeners.

11 riot shields, truncheons, and you're not doing nothing –
12 you're only trying to get down to the tube and go home.
13 So what do they do? You're walking by
14 and they're pushing you with their truncheons
15 and they start hitting the odd punk here and there.

The speaker uses "you" to broaden the account and make it relevant for anyone – this could happen to anyone. Apparently "walking by" attracted the violence.

17 The punks rebel – they don't like getting hit

18 in the face with a truncheon, nobody does.
19 So what do you do?
20 You push the copper back and what happens?

Line 17 is the punks reaction, described as a rebellion (reactive) – which is the first active involvement the punks have displayed (Widdicome & Wooffitt, 1990, 1995).

"Language may be thought of as providing the essentials of our meaning-making practices." - Tuffin (2005)

Discourse Analysis Exercise

This extract has been taken from a small focus group of men who were discussing "fighting". The speaker talks about a situation involving his niece (Alice) and her boyfriend (Steve).

Go through the text, look for anything that stands out, any play on words, and analyse for any clues that you think may be deceitful. This is an exercise solely for the practice, and there are no model answers or suggestions in the back of the book.

1 I can remember coming home one day and Alice was crying – holding her face
2 and shit and I said – you know – what's wrong with you? It sort of took me a
3 while to get the truth out of her, but what had happened was Steve had got
4 pissed off you know some guy just a friend of Alice's had run up and she'd
5 been talking to him for ages and Steve had gone off his nut and hit her – and it
6 was like where is this guy. I was really pissed off and was thinking where is
7 this guy and thought he'd gone home.
8 I went around to his house, knocked on the door and he answered and I
9 dragged him outside and you know sort of grabbed him and said do you think
10 you're fucking tough, you know he said no sort of bull shitting to me and I
11 said you know do you think you're pretty tough and gave a good sort of smack
12 in the head and said you know do you want some more sort of thing. Do you

13 like hitting girls and gave him another couple of smacks and um
    and his
14 mother sort of came out and started going off her nut at me and
    started having
15 a go at me. She knew who I was, she asked what I was doing
    and um I said he
16 beat my niece up and she just looked at him and said oh well.
17 So I just sort of left him there – he felt pretty stink. I don't think he
    would
18 have done it after that, but yeah, that's probably the only real
    time I've gone
19 out and just you know just hit somebody.

Introduction to SCAN

Building upon discourse analysis, Scientific Content Analysis (SCAN) was developed by Israeli police lieutenant and polygraph examiner Avioam Sapir. The underlying assumption of SCAN is that a statement that is recalled from an *actual experience* differs in content and quality from a statement based upon lies. This is done by analysing the written statements of suspects, and (as with any form of discourse analysis) it is important that the statements reflect the suspect's own words – either transcribed or statements they have written themselves (Vrij, 2012).

SCAN Principle (1): Denial of Allegations

Suspects who are not guilty are more likely to include denials in their statements than deceptive suspects, such as; "I did not..." or "I didn't".

Tip: The SCAN process ignores any differences between contracted and non-contracted denials.

SCAN Principle (2): Social Introduction

How are the people described in the written statement introduced? For example; "My wife Bridget..." is very clear, however when the writer is ambiguous and / or fails to introduce someone it is considered in this principle that the writer's mind prevented them from introducing the other person; such as; "We went to the party" without introducing who "we" are. Vague introductions and statements that refer to "he" or "she" (or the suddenly absence of the use of a name) can be considered suspicious and could indicate that the writer is hiding something or may indicate anxiety between the people referred to and the writer.

SCAN Principle (3): Spontaneous Corrections

This refers to corrections in the statement, such as crossing out what has been written or corrections in the transcript. Although explanations and additions are allowed, generally examinees (exposed to the SCAN process) are instructed not to cross anything out, and failure to follow this instruction could indicate deceit.

> **Tip:** In my opinion, spontaneous corrections and additions without prompting come across as more credible, so I personally disagree with this principle.

SCAN Principle (4): Lack of Conviction or Memory

This is when the writer is vague about certain elements in the statement (such as "I believe...", "I think...", "kind of...") or when the writer reports they can't remember something.

> **Tip:** SCAN considers this suspicious, however if admission of poor memory is admitted without prompting, this could also indicate honesty.

SCAN Principle (5): Structure of the Statement

This principle refers to the balance of the statement, when it is thought that in a truthful statement the first 20% is used to describe activities leading up to the event, the following 50% to describe the relevant event, and the final 30% to discuss what happened after the event. Therefore a 10 line statement would have 2 lines of introduction, 5 lines describing the event, and 3 lines about the aftermath. It is therefore considered that the more unbalanced the structure, the greater the chance of a deceptive statement.

SCAN Principle (6): Emotions

Truthful statements are more likely to contain emotional descriptions than deceptive statements, including where in the story emotions are introduced. It is considered that liars will mention emotions just before the pinnacle of the story, whereas truth tellers are more likely to mention emotions throughout the story, but particularly after the pinnacle of the story.

SCAN Principle (7): Objective and Subjective Time

How are time periods covered in the statement? Objective time refers to the actual duration of events described in the statement, whereas subjective time refers to the amount of words spent to describe these events. In a truthful statement it is thought that the objective and subjective time will correspond with each other, unlike a deceptive statement. For example; someone devotes 7 lines in their statement for an hour period, then 3 lines to cover a 2-hour period, the objective and subjective times do not correspond.

> **Tip:** I think it necessary to add to this principle, that this will depend on whether anything of significance occurred during the length of time.

SCAN Principle (8): Out of Sequence and Extraneous Information

A difference from the chronological order of events – as well as irrelevant information that is often added to hide more important information – may be deceptive.

> **Tip:** This also clashes with some experts who consider that unstructured reproduction of events and surplus or redundant details are signs of truthfulness rather than of deception.

SCAN Principle (9): Missing Information

Has any information been left out? Examples are the use of words such as "sometime after", "finally", "later on", and "shortly thereafter".

The sentence; "She began hitting and kicking me, finally she hit me with the whole bottle" indicates that the writer doesn't want to reveal what happened in the period of time between the hitting and kicking, and the hitting with the bottle (Vrij, 2010).

SCAN Principle (10): First Person, Past Tense

How is the format of the statement written? SCAN predicts that a truthful person writes in first person singular past tense, because the writer describes an event that has taken place, such as; "I saw a man jump out the window". Any deviation from this raises suspicion with SCAN.

> **Tip:** There are examples when present tense is expected and the past tense is an indicator of deception (such as the Maxine Carr example earlier).

SCAN Principle (11): Pronouns

Pronouns in a statement tend to signal commitment, responsibility and possession (I, my, he, his, they etc). Excluding pronouns ("Left work" rather than "I left work") suggests a disinclination of the writer to commit themselves to describe the action. Swapping "I" with "we" suggests the writer is attempting to absolve personal responsibility, leaving out "my" can be denying ownership. Pronouns can also identify potential tensions in relationships, such as "my wife and I" instead of "we" can indicate a distance or tension.

SCAN Principle (12): Change in Language

A change in language (terminology and vocabulary in a statement) indicates that something has changed in the mind of the writer. For example, if a suspect refers to all conversations as "conversations" except one they describe as a "discussion", it's likely they perceive this conversation differently from the others.

> **Reading Between The Lines**
>
> It is not unusual for people to resist change. Even science – what our modern minds recognise as systemized knowledge of the world – resists change. If it was not for those who fought this resistance and had the resilience in the face of adversity, surely we would believe we live in a flat world with no light bulbs. A popular change management website suggests that there are eight main reasons why people resist change, which included changing the status quo. It is this that I shall call one of "sciences deadliest of sins" – mainstream science's fear that change may cause anarchised upheaval, whereas what this resistance really manifests itself as is inadvertent stagnation of the lakes of science when there should be the flowing rivers of shared knowledge. The cry of the dinosaur that resists change echoes the quote; "If it ain't broke, don't fix it", implying that it is a mistake to try to improve something that already works. It is with this concept I shall delve into the social sciences – in particular – mainstream social psychology.

This resistance to change is clearly visible in mainstream social psychology (Tuffin, 2005). While there has been some extraordinary insights gained from social psychology experiments (such as the bystander effect and conformity), the time to call these experiments (as the most accurate) is coming to an end. Without the experiment, mainstream social psychology may struggle to find data with which to analyse, scrutinize and number crunch into meaningful statistics. The restrictive boundaries experiments place on mainstream social psychology includes a much higher chance of artificial cause and effects, distrust from participants, and a vast array of issues with ethics (Tuffin, 2005). Parker and Shotter (1990) amongst others suggest there is also the potential for experimenter bias, by saying; "...there is always the possibility that one is investigating fictions of one's own making," (Parker & Shotter, 1990, p. 109). It is no wonder that data may become scarce for the positivist mainstream social psychological perspective – even for such social animals as human beings. It is also no wonder that the "old ways" are defended, for any challenge on the experiment is a challenge to the status quo.

Let me say that experiments certainly have their place, however there is still the gaping hole left by the single-minded positivism approach to fill. And if experiments are so potentially unreliable for analysing spontaneous human interaction, where will social psychologists receive their data from? Looking from the social constructionism perspective there is however a rich amount of social psychological data right under everyone's noses – quite literally – the language that comes out of our mouths and discourse analysis. "...it is the language they [participants] speak that is the site of investigation," (Widdicombe, 1993, p. 109).

Positivism – the philosophy of science as led by empirical experimentation within psychology – requires a single truth to be discovered or achieved through objective and unbiased observation and statistical validity (Tuffin, 2005). This, as well as and seeking statistical significance is where mainstream social psychology sits quite comfortably. As a virtual polar opposite, social constructionists allow for multiple truths (as each individual maintains their own reality, their own perspective of which is true to them), frowns upon the issues listed earlier that come with amalgamating people and experiments, and is focused on the importance of linguistics as opposed to merely relying on the occularcentralistic "viewpoint". Potter (1996) suggests that – rather than regarding language as a mirror that purely reflects reality as mainstream social psychology tends to – choose to see language as a building site that allows for the construction of reality (it produces things). One of the key forms of exercising this critical social psychology is through discourse analysis, as this fully enables the educated analyst to understand our social world through language, the raw data of talk and text (Tuffin, 2005).

"Reality is in some part created by the manner in which an account is put together," (Tuffin, 2005, p. 92). Discourse analysis follows the assumption that language is action orientated (it does things), and implicated in social outcomes through how the construction, function and variability of how an account has been assembled.

In conclusion, although discourse analysis may be considered labour intensive (Gill, 1993), I believe the inclusion and acceptance this technique into mainstream social psychology would strengthen social psychology as a whole.

References

Gill, R. (1993). Justifying injustice: Broadcasters' accounts of inequality in radio. In E. Burman & I. Parker (Eds.), *Discourse Analytic Research. Repertoires and readings of Texts in Action* 75-93. London: Routledge.

Idioms, *if it ain't broke, don't fix it.* Retrieved May 7, from http://idioms.thefreedictionary.com/if+it+ain't+broke,+don't+fix+it

Parker, I. & Shooter, J. (1990). *Deconstructing Social Psychology.* London and New York: Routledge.

Potter, J. (1996). *Representing reality: Discourse, rhetoric and social construction.* London: Sage.

Reasons For Resistance To Change. Retrieved May 7, from http://www.change-management-coach.com/resistance_to_change.html

Tuffin, K. (2005). *Understanding Critical Social Psychology.* London: Sage.

Widdicombe, S. (1993). Autobiography and change: Rhetoric and authenticity of 'Gothic' style. In E. Burman & I. Parker (Eds.), *Discourse Analytic Research. Repertoires and readings of Texts in Action* 94-113. London: Routledge.

Wikipedia, *Sherlock Holmes (2009 film).* Retrieved May 7, from http://en.wikiquote.org/wiki/Sherlock_Holmes_(2009_film)

CHAPTER 14
All About Lying

""All truths are easy to understand once they are discovered;
the point is to discover them." - Galileo

Introduction

We have now covered all of the channels of communication; the areas through which the leakage of behavioural cues emerge. Before delving further into detecting deception, let us first determine exactly what constitutes a lie, explore the main motivations behind lying, how it is possible to catch a liar, and finally some precautions in detecting deceit.

The First Time I Was Truly Deceived

I am sure we all have our own stories from childhood as to when it happened – the day we stopped being innocent trusting children and became more wary of what people say – the day when we were first truly deceived.

Mine was while I was living in Auckland. I would have been 8 or 9 years old, and near to the local golf course. Closest to the edge of our property was a knee-deep swamp with thick reeds, and a bush area beside it which was great for making forts. My older brother and I would love to run around the golf course, explore, avoid being hit by flying golf balls, and wade through the swamp in bare feet looking for golf balls.

This is where our first business started – selling golf balls back to the golfers for .50c each (which was quite a lot for a child back then!). Of course my brother Matt would never share the found golf balls – or the profits – so it was up to me to earn my own money. I spent a number of hours wading through the particularly unpleasant waters bare foot – hoping not to stand on something sharp – clutching my plastic bread bag for the found golf balls. I then went home and cleaned them.

Finally I got to a grand total of 30 freshly polished golf balls! I couldn't believe it – that was $15 right there! All I had to do was find a golfer who would buy them. So off I went, my brother Matt forced to go with me so I didn't get abducted or something, and finally I found a pair of golfers who voiced interest. One in particular, a man in his early twenties perhaps, eagerly eyed the bulging plastic bag I was having difficulties in manoeuvring. However, he didn't have any money on

---

him at the time. He promised me that if I gave him the golf balls now, he'd meet me back at that very spot at 4pm the next day. As even more evidence that this adult was telling the truth; he gave me a little kiwi pin. "Make sure you bring this back tomorrow, it's precious and I want it back," he'd said. My brother wasn't interested at all – technically if my sale went through I'd have the bragging rights of selling the most golf balls between us.

Well, you can probably guess already that the man never showed up at 4pm the following day – nor the day after that – or after that... It took me a week of tears from being ripped off by an adult before the first signs of cynicism and distrust began to enter my mind. Adults can lie. I knew that kids could – my brother and I were always trying to get out of trouble – but adults too...?

From that moment onwards I became much more wary and mistrusting. So the seed was planted to learn how to never be deceived again.

The Science of Detecting Deception Through Behavioural Cues

Due to such extensive research on the science of detecting deception through behavioural cues, it is possible for a trained individual to analyse behaviour (usually video footage to enable empirical investigation) and make an accurate assessment of an individual's truthfulness (Frank, Feeley, Servoss, & Paolantonio, 2004). Although there are behavioural cues to lying, I have already mentioned that there is no single sign of deceit itself, there are only clues. It is these clues (also called cues) which trained individuals are able to identify into clusters of information. Although facial expressions alone can provide some insight, it is only when combined with the rest of the behavioural cues that we get a more complete story.

What is Lying?

Definitions of Lying

The formal definition of lying sourced from dictionary.reference.com is:

noun
1. a false statement made with deliberate intent to deceive; an intentional untruth; a falsehood.

2. something intended or serving to convey a false impression; imposture: *His flashy car was a lie that deceived no one.*
3. an inaccurate or false statement.
4. the charge or accusation of lying: *He flung the lie back at his accusers.*

verb (used without object)
5. to speak falsely or utter untruth knowingly, as with intent to deceive.
6. to express what is false; convey a false impression.

verb (used with object)
7. to bring about or affect by lying (often used reflexively): *to lie oneself out of a difficulty; accustomed to lying his way out of difficulties.*

Idioms
8. give the lie to,
a. to accuse of lying; contradict.
b. to prove or imply the falsity of; belie: *His poor work gives the lie to his claims of experience.*
9. lie in one's throat / teeth, to lie grossly or maliciously: *If she told you exactly the opposite of what she told me, she must be lying in her teeth.* Also, **lie through one's teeth.**

Dr Paul Ekman simplifies lying (2009) from the broader dictionary definition* to;

> *"Lying is the deliberate choice to mislead a target without giving any notification of the intent to do so."*

This is made up of two parts:
1) <u>Concealment</u>:   Leaving out true information.
2) <u>Falsification</u>:   Presenting false information as if it were true.
*This excludes permission for deception e.g. actors and their audience

Pam Meyer (2010) refers to the scientific definition of a lie in her book, drawn from the combined works of Vrij, *Detecting Lies and Deceit*, Ekman, *Telling Lies*; and DePaulo, *Cues to Deception*. The definition is:

> *"A lie is a message knowingly transmitted to another person with the intent to foster false beliefs or conclusions and without prior notification of purpose."*

I prefer this last definition as it covers all the points; the *intention* (a message knowingly transmitted to another person), *concealment* and *falsification* (with the intent to foster false beliefs or conclusions), to an unwilling party (without prior notification of purpose).

In order to better understand how to detect deception through the five channels of communication, the next step it to understand what constitutes a lie – what must it have in order to exist?

Include a False Statement or Representation

For a lie to include a false statement or representation would likely be one of the most obvious examples. This is when someone states, infers, claims, or merely allows the continuation of incorrect thinking of something that is not true, through their words, actions, or inactions.

> **Tip:** An example of this occurring professionally could be a real estate agent being aware of an issue with a property being sold and choosing not to tell prospective buyers. This would be making a false representation through inaction, and is of course illegal.

For a Lie to Exist it Must Have a Recipient

In order for a lie to exist, someone has to be "lied to" – in other words – there must be a recipient of an untruth in order for a lie to exist.

> **Tip:** There must be a recipient of an untruth in order for a lie to exist; otherwise it is just self deception. If I say that I am the King of England to someone else, it is a lie. If I only say it to myself, I am only deceiving myself and being seen as delusional.

A Lie Requires the Intent to Deceive

A lie is a message knowingly transmitted to another person with the intent to foster false beliefs or conclusions and without prior notification of purpose

Take another read of the definition of lying, and you will notice that it covers a great deal. The next thing that a lie requires in order to exist is the intention to deceive, mislead, omit, etc.

> **Tip:** There must be intent to deceive in order for a lie to exist; otherwise it is just an honest mistake.

"When the stakes are high, liars betray their lie by leakage of clues across multiple channels that come across as a complicated mass of signals. Adequately processing this stream of information is compounded by the investigator typically focusing on inconsistencies in the stories being told, rather than the way the stories are told. The problem with the primary focus on the story is that the liar is also focusing on presenting a consistent, albeit false, story. This is ironic in that the liar is also wrestling with his or her emotions and thoughts, and actively trying to manage their expression through the face, body, voice tone, verbal style, and words – all while monitoring the reaction of the investigator to the liar's story! This is what allows reliable cues to lies pop out in the verbal and non-verbal leakage, which investigators often don't notice because they are so attuned to the stories." (Matsumoto, p.3, *FBI Law Enforcement Bulletin*, June 2011).

"When a fact appears to be opposed to a long train of deductions, it invariably proves to be capable of bearing some other interpretation." - Sherlock Holmes

Motivations for Lying

Attempting to understand why people lie takes another step towards getting in the mind of a liar. No matter whether the lie is a small white lie or a billion dollar one, most deception stems from one or more of the following motives.

Avoid Being Punished or To Avoid Embarrassment

To avoid being punished is the most frequently mentioned motive by either children or adults (Ekman, 2009).

> **Tip:** A child claiming that they didn't break something so they didn't get into trouble is one example. Another is being caught by the police and claiming innocence (when this is not the case). Several examples of lying to avoid embarrassment could be lying about previous poor relationships or making up a story as to why someone was late.

Obtain a Reward

This motivation covers any lies used to receive some kind of reward that would otherwise be challenging (if not impossible) to achieve. To obtain a reward not otherwise readily obtainable is the second most commonly mentioned motive, by both children and adults (Ekman, 2009).

> **Tip:** Lying about how fast someone can run in order to gain credit or attention is an example. Others include a child claiming false achievements to parents of things that happened at school, any lying that occurs throughout job interviews and on resumes, and any deception that happens during a negotiation or sale, in order for the transaction to go through, are all examples.

Gain Advantage

To gain advantage over another person or over a situation is another motivator for lying.

> **Tip:** An example of this could be an advertising company faking interest in purchasing another advertising company in order to look at sensitive information they wouldn't otherwise have had access to.

Create a Positive Impression

Lies during job interviews could fit into this category, along with lying about ones appearance, job and education on dating sites.

> **Tip:** The temptation to lie to create a more positive impression can occur amongst friends, colleagues, employers, dates... Pretty much anywhere people interact in any form, online or in person; people lie to make themselves sounds better.

Controlling Information

It is said that information is power, and those controlling the information are in the position to share or withhold this information with whomever they chose.

> **Tip:** Examples of this could include a co-worker deliberately not alerting their competition of a received fax or a change of appointment, providing the wrong information prior to an appointment, or even a jealous friend not passing on a message.

Protecting Another

This motivation for lying is to protect another person from harm or punishment, with the sole motivation being to protect that person.

> **Tip:** Examples of this would be to take the blame for another's mistake, or to provide a false alibi in order to protect someone else.

Protecting Yourself from Physical or Emotional Harm

This motivation covers lies that a person makes when protecting themselves emotionally or physically.

> **Tip:** Lies to protect oneself from physical harm could be: "My husband will be home anytime," or "I'm warning you, I know martial arts". Lies to protect oneself from emotional harm are usually lies about feelings, such as playing down being hurt by a partner by sating, "I'm fine, really."

Escaping an Awkward Situation

More common than one may think – these escapes are aimed to avoid or to bring an unwanted situation to a close, from parents making up a reason why their child can not do something, to a chairman using irrelevant notes brought in by their secretary as an excuse to bring a meeting to a close earlier.

> **Tip:** There are countless examples of escaping an awkward social situation, such as looking at your watch and saying you have to go, inventing a fake appointment, pretending to have another call come through, lying about poor reception coverage, babysitter issues to avoid an event, etc.

Maintain Privacy

The motivation of lying to maintain privacy is usually justified with an excuse such as; "It's none of their business," or "If they really knew me they'd know better." In business this is one of the prime motivations (along with avoiding embarrassment) behind covering the real reason someone may have resigned or been fired.

Tip: Examples of this motivation for lying includes lying about being busy to cover the loss of driver's license or lack of money, and lying about feeling healthy to cover up an illness.

In order for society to continue to tick along as normal, it requires levels of politeness that are often untrue. These include things such as shop keepers wishing you a great day – when in fact – it is likely that they could not care less. They are told they have to say that. Salespeople working in clothing stores are reported to lie about how great something looks on a customer, and when faced with doubt by the customer, they offer another product to complete the look. The rules of politeness also tend to apply for most relationships (although not all) as most are unequipped to deal with radical honesty from their partner, expecting certain comforts, support and reassurances, whether they are true or not.

In my opinion, the only profession we willing give permission to be lied to are actors. By them being actors, we know we are being lied to in a movie; therefore the prior notification withdraws it from being a lie. Politicians do not give notice and therefore any deliberate untruth is a lie.

Some Useful Distinctions on Lying

Here are some additional useful distinctions to be aware of as you learn more about micro expressions, body language, and detecting deception (Ekman, 2009):

- Secrecy is not a lie, as saying something is a secret is acknowledging concealment.
- A broken promise is not a lie unless the promise was made knowing at the time it was untrue or unable to be kept.
- Failure to remember is not a lie, although liars may try to claim memory failure to cover their lies if discovered.
- False accounts may not be a lie, as it is quite possible for people to misinterpret events, the meaning of other people's actions, and the motives that lead people to act one way or another. Chapter 17 will go into more detail on memory.
- Natural performers have the ability to almost become the role they are playing and to virtually believe whatever they are saying. Due to believing they are saying the truth, they come across as completely credible. I also put sociopaths and psychopaths into this category – more on them at the end of the chapter.

- Over time someone can also believe their own lie and appear truthful through <u>repetitions</u> and constant <u>elaborations</u>.

Five Lying Myths

1) Touching the Face: Not only is body language the least reliable channel of predicting if someone is lying, manipulators / pacifiers are something liars may know about and try not to do.

2) Eye Contact: Studies have shown people who lie actually make more eye contact (than their usual baseline), checking to see if you believe them or not.

3) Moving & Fidgeting: You might be naturally "fidgety" or it could indicate you're experiencing elevated stress – which still doesn't mean you're lying – only that you are experiencing stress.

4) Pausing & Speech Dis-fluencies: Without knowing an individual's baseline and being aware of the context, people can mistake these for signs of deceit. Are they having to think hard, or are they under stress? This alone is not enough.

5) Poor Memory: If someone can't recall an event, it doesn't mean they're lying. People can forget things – what to look out for is how convenient it may be to forget these specific details.

Why Lies Fail

There are three major reasons for why lies fail; the fear of being caught (also referred to as detection apprehension), the subject feeling guilty about misleading the target (also referred to as deception guilt), and delight at the target believing their lie (also referred to as duping delight).

Detection Apprehension

Detection apprehension is exactly that: an apprehension or fear of the liar (subject) having their lie discovered. Even simpler, detection apprehension is being scared of being caught.

Tip: In my opinion, the best way to look for detection apprehension is to note any subtle facial expressions that indicate fear (Chapter 7).

Deception Guilt

Deception guilt is when the liar (subject) shows signs of feeling guilty about lying to the target (interviewer). In other words, they are feeling bad about lying.

> **Tip:** Guilt can often look like sadness, so note any subtle facial expressions that indicate sadness (Chapter 6).

Duping Delight

Duping delight is when a liar is secretly extremely pleased that their lie is being believed, and their delight leaks through in the form of suppressed smiling.

> **Tip:** Duping delight can be difficult to notice. To me duping delight comes across as more of a smug or contemptuous look, so keep an eye out for inappropriate smirks, often masked with a blank expression, or an emotion that best suits the situation (such as showing sadness if that's the most appropriate emotion for the liar to demonstrate).

Autonomic Nervous System Clues

The autonomic nervous system (ANS) produces changes in the body with emotional arousal, such as the frequency of breathing and swallowing, amount of sweating, changes in the face (including expressions, blushing, pupil dilation), and skin temperature changes. These changes happen involuntarily when an emotion is aroused, and are very challenging to control, which makes them very reliable clues to deceit. The polygraph measures these ANS changes, however it does not take into account why an emotion is being felt – only that an emotion / high stress / anxiety is being experienced at that time.

> **Where Behavioural Cues to Lying Don't Work**
>
> Behavioural cues to lying are more difficult to detect when people are not vested in having their story believed and have no fear of detection. To illustrate, I'll tell you a brief true story.
>
> The extended family all met for Christmas in 2010, and a family member of mine was interested in learning more about deception (having a business, property and negotiating background). We spoke for a little while before he said; "So I can test you then. You can tell me if I'm lying?" I responded by saying that detecting deception through the five channels of communication tend to work if there is something at stake, if he had enough motivation for me to believe his lie. I explained further that I could claim that Santa Claus came to me that morning and took me around the block on his sled – if I didn't

care if I was believed or not. If however my life depended on it (or my reputation, etc) then I would be much more invested in having my lie believed.

He responded by asking how I could demonstrate this, so I suggested that if I could pick if he was lying or not, I would get his lovely big house (where we were having Christmas dinner). After a little stuttering he smiled, having learnt the lesson.

The higher the stakes, the easier it is to identify behavioural clues to deception.

Precautions in Detecting Deception

Straight out of Paul Ekman's *Telling Lies* (Ekman, 2009) book, I have listed what I believe are the most important precautions in detecting deception:

"There are two kinds of mistakes that are exactly opposite in cause and consequence. In disbelieving-the-truth the lie catcher mistakenly judges a truthful person to be lying. In believing-a-lie the lie catcher mistakenly judges a liar to be truthful." - Dr. Paul Ekman

(1) Try to be extremely clear to yourself regarding the basis of any hunches and intuitions about whether or not someone is lying.
(2) Be aware that there are two dangers in detecting deceit: disbelieving the truth (judging a truthful person to be lying) and believing a lie (judging a liar to be truthful).
(3) The absence of a sign of deceit is not evidence of truth; some people do not leak deceptive clues. The presence of a sign of deceit is not always evidence of lying; some people appear ill-at-ease or guilty even when they are truthful.
(4) Search your mind for any preconceptions you may have about a suspect.

Preconceptions and the Confirmation Bias

Confirmation bias is the tendency for people to favour information that confirms their current beliefs, and is dangerous for someone detecting deception as they can get derailed if their opinion of a subject affects their assessments.

Sociopaths and Psychopaths

I am choosing not to delve into mental illnesses on the whole and how they could affect detecting deception; however, I will include a brief rundown on sociopaths and psychopaths – and the major differences between them. At workshops and online forums the question about the differences and how to detect deception with these individuals comes up frequently.

Definition of Sociopath and Psychopath

A sociopath is someone who is affected with a personality disorder marked by antisocial behaviour. A psychopath is a person with an antisocial personality disorder, manifested in aggressive, distorted, criminal, or unethical behaviour without empathy or remorse.

Another Teen Murder, Watch For The Signs

"A Texas teenager allegedly shot his mother and younger sister dead before calling 911 to recount the murders. Speaking in a soft, calm voice Jake Evans, 17, told the 911 operator he had been 'kind of planning on killing for a while now', *Fox News* reports.

"He said he had used a .22 revolver to kill his 15-year-old sister and 48-year-old mother in their Parker County home early Friday morning."
(Source Article: http://news.msn.co.nz/worldnews/8544097/texas-teen-murders-family-calls-911)

Evans states that he didn't know why he killed his mother and sister, however he did say; **"I've been kind of planning on killing for a while now."**

According to Arrigo & Shipley (2005), these types of incidents don't just come out of the blue – there are signs. These signs may be extremely obvious to an outsider, social worker or teacher etc, however may be more challenging to acknowledge by family members and close friends – written off as; "Oh, that's just them." In many of these scenarios the juvenile that appears to kill for no reason at all has in fact discussed their urges with someone previously, such as a counsellor. In some way, these "advance confessions" could allow the troubled individual to go on to kill without worry as they "should have been stopped" or some similar excuse.

I'd be interested to know if Jake Evans was already known to be a risk, whether he had discussed his urges with anyone. Hindsight can be 20/20 – however we want to develop a more accurate foresight – prevention is the best form of risk management. People are stereotypically more wary of outsiders, and yet some of the biggest threats can come from within the family unit. Here are some interesting statistics:

- In 1988, 16% of all murders were committed against family members (in the US, Bureau of Justice Statistics). This was made up of:
- 6.5% by spouses
- 3.5% by parents (Children under 5 years old murdered between 1976-2000: 31% killed by fathers, 30% mothers, 23% male acquaintance, 7% other relative & only 3% strangers - leaving 6% unlisted)
- 1.9% by their children
- 1.5% sibling violence
- 2.6% victimised by other family members

- Between 1976 – 2000, 11% of murders were committed by an intimate member of the family (US Dept of Justice, 2002).

- 40% of all homicides in the US are the result of domestic violence (Browne & Herbert, 1997).

Bottom line, watch for the signs. A "healthy paranoia" is much better in my opinion than kicking yourself with 20/20 hindsight, having ignored the clues.

What is a Serial Killer?

The term "serial killer" was first used by Robert Ressler (former FBI director of the Violent Criminal Apprehension Program) in the mid-1970s. Prior to this term, they were referred to as "crimes in a series", mass murders or stranger-on-stranger crime.

A serial killer is traditionally defined as an individual who has killed three or more people over a period of more than a month, with down time (a "cooling off period") between the murders, and whose motivation for killing is usually based on psychological gratification (Wikipedia).

What Drives a Serial Killer?

Serial killer Henry Lee Lucas blamed his upbringing; Jeffrey Dahmer claimed that he was born with a "part" of him missing. Ted Bundy claimed pornography made him do it. Herbert Mullin – Santa Cruz killer of thirteen – blamed the voices in his head that told him it was time to "sing the die song." Carl Panzram swore that prison turned him into a monster, whereas Bobby Joe Long said a motorcycle accident made him hypersexual and eventually a serial lust killer, and John Wayne Gacy believed that his victims deserved to die.
(Source http://www.trutv.com/library/crime/serial_killers/notorious/tick/victims_1.html).

Top 7 Serial Killer Myths

1) Serial killers are dysfunctional loners.
2) Serial killers are all white males.
3) Serial killers are only motivated by sex.
4) Serial killers operate interstate.
5) Serial killers can't stop killing.
6) Serial killers are insane or evil.
7) Serial killers want to get caught.
(Sourced from www.all-about-forensic-psychology.com)

Did You Know? Nostril flaring allows more air to oxygenate the body in preparation of fight or flight.

About Sociopaths and Psychopaths

A *sociopath* is someone who is affected with a personality disorder marked by antisocial behaviour. A *psychopath* is a person with an antisocial personality disorder, manifested in aggressive, perverted, criminal, or amoral behaviour without empathy or remorse.

David Lykken's studies revealed that psychopaths are born with temperamental differences that lead them to being risk seekers, impulsive, fearless as well as not being able to socialize normally. Sociopaths have normal temperaments, but their personality disorder tends to affect their lives regarding parenting, peers, and their intelligence.

Sociopaths can be anyone from your mother, father, best friend, neighbour or even your co-worker, and you would not even realise that they are dealing with this disorder that affects everything in their daily life. Sociopaths go above and beyond themselves to make sure that other people around them have no idea that their life is something other than what it is. More than likely you have met one or two sociopaths in your life and not even realise it.

Psychopaths on the other hand are usually very flamboyant with how they deal with their disorder. Some famous psychopaths are Charles Manson, Richard Ramirez, Theodore Bundy and David Berkowitz. These four men are famous for being some of the most notorious and manipulative serial killers in history. Not all psychopaths are as overt as these four men, however their rage is almost always as intense, it just depends on how they channel it. "Psychopaths are human predators who coldly, callously and ruthlessly use charm, deceit, manipulation, threats, intimidation and violence to dominate and control others and to satisfy their own selfish needs and desires." – Hare (1993)

Similar Characteristics between a Sociopath and a Psychopath

- Sociopaths are very charming. Psychopaths use superficial charm to lure their victims.
- Sociopaths can be extremely manipulative and will try to con you whenever possible. Psychopaths are very predatory and will usually live off other people.
- Sociopaths feel that they are entitled to everything. Psychopaths are extremely self-centred.
- Sociopaths will lie continuously to get what they want. They can even sometimes manipulate a lie detector. Psychopaths are very deceptive and tend to lie continuously.
- Sociopaths have no remorse, shame or guilt. Psychopaths show no remorse of guilt towards their victims.
- Sociopaths will never take blame for anything they have done to anyone no matter if it is family or friend. Psychopaths are always blaming other people for their actions.
- Sociopaths need to have excitement in their lives or live on the edge. Psychopaths must always do something to keep themselves from boredom.
- Sociopaths have many sexual partners and tend to act out many sexual acts. Psychopaths have many sexual partners in their lifetime.
- Sociopaths rarely stay in one place for long (home/work). Psychopaths are very impulsive with their lifestyle.

More Specifically Sociopathic Characteristics

- Sociopaths will show love and happiness only when it serves their purpose. None of the feelings are genuine. Sociopaths have no room for love in their life.
- Sociopaths have a lack of empathy for the pain they cause on their victims.
- Sociopaths believe that they are all mightier than thou; there is no concern of how their behaviour impacts others.
- Sociopaths usually have a long history of juvenile delinquency as well as behaviour problems.
- Sociopaths will change themselves (appearance, behaviours, etc) if they know it will keep them from being found out.

More specifically Psychopath Characteristics

- Psychopaths never have a realistic view of their lives. (King of the World, from another planet, etc)
- Psychopaths always want psychological gratification in sexual and criminal activities.
- Psychopaths tend to try suicide, rarely succeeding.

(Collated by Jeanne Marie Kerns)

CHAPTER 15
Deception Detection 101

"And how can you possibly know that I have told a lie?"
"Lies, my dear boy, are found out immediately, because they are
of two sorts. There are lies that have short legs, and lies that
have long noses. Your lie, as it happens, is one of those that
have a long nose." - Pinocchio (1892)

Introduction

The last chapter was designed to increase your understanding of what makes up a lie, what kinds of lies there are, the beginnings of how to catch a liar, and some precautions before you get too far into deception detection. It is easy to misinterpret or ignore clues to deceit, however it is my intention that after reading this book and doing the exercises, using online micro expressions training, and practicing your skills you will massively increase your ability to spot a liar and become more proficient with the dangers of misjudging a lie; whether it be disbelieving the truth or believing a lie. The final piece of the puzzle to detecting deception is to practice with videos.

This chapter introduces some of the common terminology and asks what behaviours betray a lie. Research indicates that it is not just the presence or absence of behavioural cues that indicate lying; it is how these non-verbal cues vary from a person's baseline and how they blend with what is being said that makes them excellent clues to deception. When behavioural cues are analysed, accuracy in determining the truth from lying increases much higher than the average person, with the average person spotting lies not much better than chance (Frank, 2009; Frank, O' Sullivan, & Menasco, 2009).

Do Men Lie More Often Than Women?

Men and women actually tend to lie about the same amount of time as each other, however it's what they lie about that differs. Men lie to make themselves look better in the eyes of others, while women tend to lie to spare feelings and make other people feel better.

Why Learn How to Detect Lies?

Research has shown that a normal everyday person will lie on average 3 times for every 10 minutes of conversation – bearing in mind that a lot of these lies are social ones, such as answering; "I'm fine thanks," when the person really isn't, or "Yes, you look lovely in that". Keeping this in mind, the average untrained individual has around 54% chance of catching lies. There is so much fraud, theft, identity theft, embezzlement, information leaks, false qualifications and documentations...then there are the lies closer to home. Relationships, children, parents... The list goes on and on. The better question to ask is; "How much could it cost you *not* to learn how to detect lies?"

Did You Know? Neck-ties were originally worn by Roman soldiers as either part of a uniform or as a symbol that they were a part of a particular group. The modern neck-tie descended from the cravat around the 17th-century. In 1646, when Louis XIV was 7 years old he began wearing a lace cravat – which set the fashion for French nobility. These were the beginning of intricate lace cravats. Then, as the modern age approached, and the neck-tie was required to become easier to put on – and comfortable to wear all day – the longer thinner neck-tie was introduced.

Common Terminology

Throughout the book so far I have used terms such as baselining and clusters with minor explanations – now I will explain what I believe to be the most common deception detection terminology.

Baseline

Baselining behaviour – also referred to as benchmarking behaviour – is identifying what is normal behaviour for a subject. Finding a baseline is to find the subject's neutral or normal state of behaviour. In order to identify anything out of the ordinary or out of character, one must first identify the ordinary. Do they have any particular idiosyncrasies in their typical behaviour? Pay attention in order to avoid making the Brokaw Hazard (described below).

Tip: Some ideas for what to look for when baselining someone's behaviour include paying attention to the person's reactions, gestures and habits, posture and standing or sitting position, and how they talk (fast or slow, pauses or stutters, etc).

Once you have an idea of how the person acts "normally", pay attention to anything that changes. For example, you are having a conversation with a co-worker named John. His baseline in the tea room is a cheerful attitude, he speaks quickly, and sits forwards in his chair with one arm resting on the table and the other free for his coffee and to illustrate and gesture. Part way through the conversation you bring up the topic of a recent theft, and immediately John leans back, crosses his arms and begins to talk slower and his mood darkens. This alone doesn't mean he's lying; however it *is* a large variation from his baseline.

Cluster

A cluster of cues relates to not just one or two clues to deceit occurring within close proximity to one another, but three or more. Clusters, or hot spots, are extremely likely areas where the subject is being deceitful.

Tip: Following on from the baseline example, John showed a cluster of clues that were far from his baseline; he leaned back, crossed his arms, talked slower and his emotion changed. This group of four clues becomes a cluster or hot spot of clues as there are three or more variations from the baseline.

Disbelieving the Truth Error

Very simply put, disbelieving the truth is where the target (or interviewer) consciously or unconsciously mistakes an error and incorrectly judges a truthful person to be lying. These errors can occur due to the Othello Error (see below for a full explanation), examining the wrong cues (where the interviewer follows incorrect myths or beliefs about how liars should act), neglect of interpersonal differences (see below for the Brokaw Hazard explanation), heuristics (the use of these mental shortcuts can lead to errors and biases when detecting deception), poor interviewing (see Chapter 17 for more on memory and interviewing) and over-estimating lie catching tools (all deception detection tools and techniques have errors, yet practitioners can ignore these errors and consider the tools infallible) (Ekman, 2009; Vrij, 2010).

Tip: Another way to explain the disbelieving-the-truth error is accusing someone who is genuinely telling the truth as being a liar.

Believing a Lie Error

A believing a lie error is where the interviewer mistakenly believes a subject (or liar) to be truthful. This type of error can occur for many different reasons, such as: The Ostrich Effect (people not being motivated to detect the deception as it is not in their best interests to do so), the <u>absence of Pinocchio's nose</u> (lie detection is challenging as most people are only able to detect lies about half the time – there are no set behavioural clues, physiological clues or speech patterns that are specifically related to deception), <u>subtle differences</u> (the difference between the truth or a lie might be the slightest most subtle variance from the baseline that this is too hard to notice), <u>countermeasures</u> (liars may take steps to appearing more believable), <u>embedded lies</u> (when the liar embeds a lie into an otherwise truthful story), <u>lack of feedback</u> (this is the lack of feedback for the interviewer as to how accurate their lie detecting skills are in relativity), <u>following conversation rules</u> (these rules hint that in normal conversations it is not polite to continue to ask someone to elaborate and ask further questions, and it is expected people will look each other in the eyes – both of which are counter-productive to catching a liar) and finally there are just <u>good liars</u> (liars who are extremely challenging to detect are people whose natural behaviour appears honest, who are not cognitively challenged to lie, and those who do not feel detection apprehension, deception guilt or duping delight when lying – see Chapter 14 for more) (Vrij, 2010).

> **Tip:** The exact opposite of the disbelieving the truth error, the believing a lie error is when the interviewer believes a liar's story.

Othello Error

The Othello Error (also referred to as a preconception or confirmation bias) is a disbelieving-the-truth error when the interviewer fails to consider that a truthful person who is under stress may appear to be lying.

The name of this error comes from Shakespeare's *Othello*, when Othello accuses Desdemona of loving Cassio and demands she confess. Desdemona asks that Cassio be called to testify to her innocence, however Othello tells her he's already had Cassio murdered. Desdemona realises she will not be able to prove her innocence and that Othello will kill her. Othello interprets Desdemona's fear and distress as guilt, thus (falsely) confirming his belief that she was unfaithful. He failed to see that if she were innocent she would show the same emotions (Ekman, 2009).

> **Tip:** The Othello Error is a truthful subject fearing being disbelieved, and this fear is misidentified as being detection apprehension.

Brokaw Hazard

When Tom Brokaw was the interviewer on NBC TV's "Today Show," he described how he detected deception; "Most of the clues I get from people are verbal, not physical. I don't look at a person's face for signs that he is lying. What I'm after are convoluted answers or sophisticated evasions." The Brokaw Hazard is the failure to take into account how people differ in expressing themselves, people's individual differences. Lie catchers are particularly vulnerable to the Brokaw Hazard when they are unacquainted with the suspect, not familiar with idiosyncrasies in the suspect's typical behaviour. Due to this error in lie catching, I need to stress once more the importance of gaining a baseline on a subject. Ideally this should eliminate or greatly reduce the Brokaw Hazard (Ekman, 2009).

Tip: The Brokaw Hazard is the failure to take into account that people are unique, individual, and will express themselves differently. Lie catchers are particularly vulnerable to the Brokaw Hazard when they are unacquainted with the subject – mostly due to not having benchmarked the behaviour and therefore not familiar with the personal idiosyncrasies.

Slip of the Tongue

In *The Psychopathology of Everyday Life* Sigmund Freud showed how the faulty actions of everyday life (such as slips of the tongue, the forgetting of familiar names, and mistakes in reading and writing) were not accidents but meaningful events revealing internal psychological conflicts. "Slips express", he said, "…something one did not wish to say: it becomes a mode of self-betrayal."

Tip: Put very simply, I look at the slip of the tongue as an unintentional mistake with speech. For example, Ted Kennedy made an interesting slip of the tongue in a televised speech; "Our national interest ought to be to encourage the *breast* and brightest…" Another excellent example is by former US President George H.W. Bush; "For seven and a half years I've worked alongside President Reagan. We've had triumphs. Made some mistakes. We've had some sex…uh…setbacks."

Ground Truth

Ground truth is *knowing* what the truth is, and relates to the issue of not knowing whether someone is lying or telling the truth independently of lie detecting techniques and tools (such as investigative interview, video analysis or the polygraph). Ambiguity about the ground truth is where problems arise with suspects (such as the innocent going to prison), and what many researchers and experiments on the validity of lie detecting tools fail to account for.

> **Tip:** Using the example of a murder, the ground truth is what *actually* occurred (the murder), what investigators should be searching to uncover (the murderer), and only the guilty suspects (the murderer or potentially any eye witnesses) know for sure.

What Behaviours Betray a Lie?

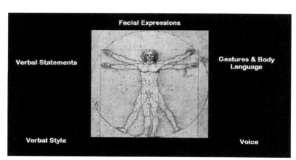

What behaviours will betray a lie? What do you look for? Summing up what has been covered in the previous chapters can be explained simply; the five channels of communication. These channels are when leakage escapes (leakage being an unintentional muscle twitch, expression gesture, voice pitch, the way something is stated – put another way – the leak or variation from the baseline): <u>facial expressions</u>, <u>gestures and body language</u>, <u>voice</u>, <u>verbal style</u>, and <u>verbal statements</u>.

The channels of communication are important for detecting deception as these are where the clues are deception leak from. As I have said before, any one clue can not determine deception, which is why you must look for a cluster of cues. Then the trick is to avoid jumping to conclusions. For example, a man is being questioned about the whereabouts of his teenage step daughter. As he answers "I don't know where she is," he flashes a micro expression of fear, crosses his arms and legs then leans back. Does this mean he is lying? Even though there were several cues clustered together, we do not know *why*. We must consider other potential reasons of why he acted this way: perhaps he argued with his wife to allow his step daughter more freedom and feels guilty about this. Or it could also mean that he killed her and dumped her body. The point here is, **do not jump to conclusions**. Just because a cluster of cues were seen does not instantly mean someone is lying.

> **Tip:** An example I use regularly during workshops is displaying contempt. If I shake my head, lean back with a sign and flash contempt, it could be related to what was happening (such as a conversation). If this is the case, then something that was said potentially annoyed me quite a bit. However, we must also consider the idea that I just remembered that I had forgotten to bring an important document from the office and it's still sitting on my desk. I feel contempt towards my self ("How could I have forgotten such an important document?") – However observers are completely unaware of this internal dialogue.
>
> This is why it's important to confirm, ask further questions and don't jump to conclusions. Perhaps ask, "Is something wrong?" to allow the potential for a truthful answer to be revealed.

What Else To Look For

Once you have established a baseline, be aware of any behaviour that seems outside of the norm, including (but not limited to) body language that indicates negative emotions and emblems. Remember that manipulators often increase when someone is uncomfortable and / or lying, and illustrators decrease due to lines not being rehearsed or experiencing a high cognitive load. Some liars tend to withdraw, almost as if they are trying to take up less space. Common manipulators of a liar include touching the face, mouth, eyes, ears, and sometimes the hair.

> **Asymmetrical Expressions**
>
> Asymmetrical expressions are where the same expression appears on both sides of the face; however the expression is stronger on one side. This is a clue that the emotions being displayed are not likely to be genuine, with the exception of contempt (which is the only genuine expression that is asymmetrical) (Ekman, 2009). Also, facial expressions that are not synchronized with body movements are likely to be deception clues.

There is no evidence to say that liars avoid making eye contact, in fact often the opposite is the case. There is also no scientific evidence linking where a subject's eyes look for recall or make-believe.

CHAPTER 16
The Three Steps to Detecting Deception

"Nonverbal communication and lying are more complicated by
the fact there are no clear-cut guaranteed clues to deceit"
- Frank & Svetieva (2012)

Introduction

As it can be confusing and take a little while to become proficient with the details of detecting deception through behavioural cues, this chapter is dedicated to simplifying everything that has been discussed thus far. Everything we have covered is based upon research, and it is due to this research on the science of detecting deception that we know it is possible for trained individuals to analyse behaviour and make accurate assessments of an individual's truthfulness (Frank, Feeley, Servoss, & Paolantonio, 2004).

The Three Steps to Detecting Deception

The simplest way I can explain detecting deception is in three steps – bearing in mind that behavioural cues to lying are different when people are not invested in having their story believed and / or have no fear of detection (Ekman, 2009; Matsumoto, 2011).

Step 1) Obtain a Baseline

Baselining behaviour – also referred to as benchmarking behaviour – is identifying what is normal behaviour for a subject. Finding a baseline is to find the subject's neutral or normal state of behaviour. In order to identify anything out of the ordinary or out of character (clues to deceit), one must first identify the ordinary. Are there any particular idiosyncrasies in the subject's typical behaviour?

Other normal behaviour clues are also important, including gestures, voice, and verbal style. The start, however, is always to focus on facial expressions, because the research has demonstrated that these are involuntary reactions and thus important non-verbal cues to deception (Frank & Ekman, 1997). Expressions are likely to be false when they are asymmetrical, the duration of expression is either too long or too short, or the timing of the expression in relation to the speech is not synchronized (Ekman, 2009). A mistake referred to as the Brokaw Hazard – the possibility of misjudging people's idiosyncrasies as deceit – can be avoided if a baseline is obtained (Ekman, 2009).

3 Steps to Detecting Deception

The simplest way I can explain detecting deception is in three steps – bearing in mind that behavioural cues to lying are different when people are not vested in having their story believed and have no fear of detection:

1) <u>Obtain a baseline</u>: Baselining behaviour – also referred to as benchmarking behaviour - is identifying what is normal behaviour for a subject.

Finding a baseline is to find the subject's neutral or normal state of behaviour. In order to identify anything out of the ordinary or out of character (clues to deceit), one must first identify the ordinary. Do they have any particular idiosyncrasies in their typical behaviour?

Pay attention in order to avoid making the Brokaw Hazard - the possibility of misjudging people's idiosyncrasies as deceit.

2) <u>Recognise clusters</u>: A cluster of cues relates to not just one or two clues to deceit occurring within a set event, but three or more. Clusters, or hot spots, are extremely likely areas where the subject is being deceitful.

These could be any combination of clues from the five channels of communication (face, body & gestures, voice, verbal style and statements).

3) <u>Practice and don't jump to conclusions</u>!

      - Stu Dunn

Step 2) Recognise Clusters

A cluster of clues relates to not just one or two clues of deceit occurring within a set event, but three or more. Clusters, or hot spots, are extremely likely areas where the subject is being deceitful (Ekman, 2009).

Clues to deception emerge through detection apprehension (fear of being caught), deception guilt (guilt about lying to the target) and duping delight (delight at having a lie believed). These clues generally increase if the stakes are high if they are caught, appearing as leakage across any combination of the five channels of communication; the face, body & gestures, voice, verbal style and statements (Matsumoto, 2011).

Did You Know? Micro expressions were first discovered by Haggard and Isaacs over 40 years ago. They published a report on these expressions, which they called "micromomentary" expressions in 1966. The article they wrote was entitled *Micro-momentary facial expressions as indicators of ego mechanisms in psychotherapy.* Many subsequent studies have been conducted based on the research by Haggard and Isaacs, but the discovery of micro expressions should be attributed to them.

Step 3) Practice and Don't Jump to Conclusions!

Because micro expressions, changes in body language and cues in verbal statements are subtle, they typically require focused attention to detect – and of course – practice. In many situations, the investigator is primarily focused on the story being told, and not so much how it is told and what is being shown when it is told. Multi-tasking has been shown to reduce accuracy of deception detection (Ophir, Nass, & Wagner, 2009), which challenges investigators who aim to do more than just be aware of expressions.

Individuals trained in detecting deception can make mistakes, as human beings are unpredictable, each having the possibility of acting individually within any given situation. Common errors that occur by the lie catcher could be disbelieving the truth, when the lie catcher mistakenly judges a truthful person to be lying. A version of this is the Othello Error – also referred to as a preconception or confirmation bias – which is a disbelieving the truth error when the interviewer fails to consider that a truthful person who is under stress may appear to be lying. To put more simply, the Othello Error is a truthful subject fearing being disbelieved (Ekman, 2009). A final error that I'll note to be aware of is the believing a lie error; when the lie catcher mistakenly judges a liar to be truthful (Ekman, 2009).

The SDL Detecting Deception Model

Even when placed into three steps, there are still so many things to remember when it comes to detecting deception. It is for this reason that I put together the SDL Detecting Deception Model, which provides a visual representation of everything that has been covered in the book so far. The notes in this model are very brief and are aimed to work as memory prompts. You are welcome to download this model and print it, which can be found at the following web address:

http://studunnsdl.files.wordpress.com/2013/08/sdl-deception-detection-model1.jpg

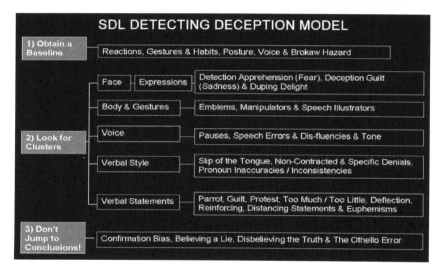

PART 3 – IMPROVING DETECTING DECEPTION SKILLS

How To Practice Detecting Deception

This is just a little guide to help give you an idea of what you can do once you have read this book and gone through the exercises (including Chapter 13's exercises testing your understanding of detecting deception in speech). One of the first things I recommend (other than continue to educate yourself on the subject) is to learn the terminology. Print out the SDL Deception Model, place it on your wall, and look up anything that you can not remember. Some people make cards for each definition, statement, expression and gesture (and even add in their own) to make a pack of informative body language cards.

The next task to master is the detection of micro and subtle expressions (there are recommendations of how to do this at the end of Chapter 2). The good news is that it does not take long to become proficient. Included in the facial expressions education, I recommend going through the smiles exercises listed in Chapter 3.

By this stage, you should be quite capable of picking live expressions and interpreting body language – which is when practicing with the exercises in this book, as well as any images uploaded to the SDL Facebook page (www.facebook.com/sdlmicroexpressions) can be of huge benefit. The reason is that it is extremely difficult to gain feedback on your interpretations when you are practicing by yourself.

> **Did You Know?** Although women are superior to men in reading non-verbal messages, they are no better then men in detecting truths and lies in strangers (DePaulo, 2003). Women are however less suspicious than men and are more inclined to believe that they are being told the truth (DePaulo, Epstein & Wyer, 1993).

Now we come to improving your ability to detect deception. I do not recommend testing your skills on your partner! My recommendation is to watch the news, reality shows, and interviews just to see what you notice. You can proactively find video clips of interviews that interest you, and analyse them yourself, then share them with others who also wish to improve their skills for comparison. Occasionally I will analyse video clips, which gives you the opportunity to do your own analyse and compare it to mine to see how you are doing.

3 year olds may lie to avoid punishment or because they've been asked to. By 4, children are capable of telling deliberate lies - Vrij (2002)

Tips for Interviewing & Video Analysis

After video analysis, the next step is live interviewing (see the next chapter for more on interviewing). Over time it is likely you will find your own style and methods of analysing video footage and interviewing, therefore what I have listed should be used as a guide or a starting point.

- In an interview, work in pairs. One person concentrates on the interview itself, and the other concentrates on observing the five channels of communication, marking behaviour and suggesting areas for the interviewer to dig deeper.
- Also in an interview setting, obtaining a video can be extremely helpful if the response to the interview is not required immediately.
- When analysing video:

STEP 1:   Some prefer to watch right through, then go back and take notes. To save time, I prefer to watch and pause as I go the first time, and make brief notes on potential events to come back to.

STEP 2:   On the second viewing, go to the areas that caught your attention and explore. What was it? Something said? A facial expression? Some body language that looked a little different? Whatever it may be, examine closer – keep what you still agree with and discard what you don't.

STEP 3:   Take a snapshot / screen dump / image of the exact frame where you see an event. Some video players have the snapshot function. Otherwise, there are free programs that can do this, such as XnView. Save each image as a .jpeg under the time stamp (e.g. Sample 00.01.58).

STEP 4:   Write your evidence / story for each image.

STEP 5:   Time permitting, I would now recommend re-watching the video in full, and make any adjustments to your analysis that you feel necessary. Remember to avoid absolutes, make any opinions clear, and try to use the terminology you have learnt.

STEP 6:   Write an overview. You should now have a good enough idea how you feel about the video, and be able to provide a clear overview. If your overview is ever challenged, you have the images and descriptions that can be used as evidence towards how you came to your conclusion.

- Remember to avoid any personal bias. You may like or dislike the subject in the interview or video, and run the danger of losing impartiality.

How Do I Deal With Liars?

I personally am not into confrontation. I alert people of what I do; "You DO know what I do, right?" If they don't, I give them a card...and watch them change. Some stay strong in their lie anyway. Here's the thing – unless I have physical evidence, I can't ever be 100% certain. So unless I have said proof – they stick to their lie – I might just let it go. However in parting I'll let them know that I'm not convinced, then do my best to drop it (if it's not too important). Kids and teenagers are different: I'm more likely to be much more direct and point out what they're doing, such as; "You know that when you turn your wrist at the same time as you step backwards suggests that you just told a lie...?"

An Example of Video Analysis

Below is an example of an analysis done around November 2011 of a clip where Robin Roberts interviews Gary Giordano over the suspicious disappearance of Robyn Gardner. The video and full analysis can be found here:

http://studunnsdl.wordpress.com/2012/09/27/analysis-of-the-gary-giordano-interview-by-robin-roberts/

Time Stamp	Description	Interpretation
00.29	This looks like a cross between duping delight and contempt during his comment on being interviewed / interrogated for 4 months, he's leaving something out.	Perhaps, if duping delight, he's hiding the fact he's got away with it. It would more likely be contempt if he is being honest.
00.59	Long winded answer to end up avoiding answering the question. Gary uses the Deflection Statement to avoid answering certain questions. He also glances to his lawyer.	The Deflection Statements are normally responses aimed to ignore or deflect questions. His glance to the lawyer could indicate a rehearsed response that he was not going to discuss what happened the day his "companion" went missing.
01.16	This is meant to be Gary's "Surprise Face" at hearing the news that there was talk about him and Robyn Gardner showing signs of drinking heavily.	I don't think this looks anything like surprise, which could indicate that he was aware of what was being discussed and faked his surprise.

PART 4

THE APPLICATION OF THE SCIENCE

CHAPTER 17
Introduction to Memory and Interviewing

"We remember what we understand; we understand only what we pay attention to; we pay attention to what we want."
- Edward Bolles

Introduction

Getting the sense of what works in the real world is what Part 4 of this book is all about. Parts 1, 2 and 3 have introduced the five channels of communication and how to detect deception through behavioural cues – Part 4 will introduce memory (and how it can affect interviews), investigative interviewing techniques, and Chapter 18 will finish off with a wide range of people's real world experiences with non-verbal communication – from a number of body language professionals to retail assistants.

An Introduction to Memory

Goldstein describes the definition of memory as "the processes involved in retaining, retrieving, and using information about stimuli, images, events, ideas, and skills after the original information is no longer present" (Goldstein 2011, p. 116). Having a basic understanding of how the memory works helps the lie catcher to become aware of some finer details that can confound even the most experienced of interviewers.

Sensation and Perception

Sensation is defined as "the conversation of energy from the environment into a pattern of response by the nervous system" Sensation is the registering of information / stimulus.

Perception is the interpretation of that information (Kalat, 2008).

The main point here is that although people may share similar sensations, it is the interpretation of these sensations where people's opinions can greatly differ. For example, what are these images of?

Do you see a young woman or an old lady? Do you see a rabbit or a duck? Do you see a candle stick or vase, or do you see two faces? Both answers are correct for each image.

Our experiences translate the stimuli of the outside world into very different representations.

Memory

Memory refers to the capacity to retain and retrieve information and provides personal identity and experiences. Memory can also be extremely selective; when remembering complex information we typically alter it in ways that helps us to make sense of the material based on what we already know – or think we know (Wade & Tavris, 2006).

Memory involves much more than taking information and storing it in a mental compartment for later use. Memory must be encoded (getting information into memory), stored (how information is maintained), and retrieved (pulling information back out of memory). There are a number of ways to improve memory, with deeper levels of processing (when something has meaning to you), elaboration (linking stimulus to other information you know), and dual-coding (receiving information visually and semantically) helping us to remember (or encode) more effectively. There are also a number of issues with memory.

Issues with Memory

Below are several examples of issues with regards to memory, when either during the encoding, storing or retrieval information is not absorbed, or it is vulnerable to change (Wade & Tavris, 2006; Weiten, 2010).

Source misattribution: The inability to distinguish an actual memory of an event from information you learned about the event elsewhere.

Flashbulb memories: Significant event (such as 9/11) when memory of the event is held in apparent photographic detail. People have a high confidence in the details of the memory; however the detail has lower accuracy than an everyday memory.

Unconscious transference: The tendency of an eyewitness to misidentify a familiar (but innocent) face as belonging to the person responsible for a crime.

Confabulation: Confusion of an event that happened to someone else with what happened to you, or a belief that you remember something when it never actually happened.

Unconscious Transference / Confabulation in Action.

An example involved Donald M. Thomson, an Australian psychologist and lawyer, who walked into a Sydney police station on routine court-related business and was arrested for assault and rape in a weird turn of events.

The evening before his arrest, Thomson appeared on a local television program, where he discussed psychological research on eyewitness testimony and how people might best remember the faces of criminals observed during a robbery. As he spoke, a Sydney woman watching the show was attacked, raped and left unconscious in her apartment. When she awoke several hours later, she called the police and named Thomson as her assailant.

The following day, after Thomson's arrest, the woman confidently selected him as the perpetrator from a lineup of possible rapists at the police station.

Thomson, of course, professed his innocence. "The police didn't believe me at first," he recalls, "but I had appeared on a live television show when the crime occurred, so I had a good alibi."

Officials quickly dropped the charges when they realised the woman had unwittingly substituted Thomson's televised face for that of the attacker. "She had apparently watched my television appearance very closely, but it's not clear if she ever saw her assailant's face," says Thomson, now at Monash University in Clayton, Australia.

Source: Eyewitness Identification, Chapter 14, Frontiers from Psychology, http://www.intropsych.com/ch14_frontiers/eyewitness_identification.html

---

Selective attention: The ability to attend to one source of information while ignoring other sources.

Divided attention: Attention is limited; therefore it has only so much "capacity" or cognitive load available to devote to mental tasks.

Attention tunnelling: All attention is focused on one thing (such as a weapon).

Suggestion: As memory is reconstructive, it is vulnerable to suggestion. Eye witnesses are particularly vulnerable to suggestion through leading questions.

Schemas: This is an organised cluster of knowledge about something based upon previous experience (such as how a doctor's office would look or how a child's birthday party might be). People are more likely to remember things that are consistent with their schemas. Stereotyping – put simply – would be the "people" version of a schema (e.g. your expectations of how a doctor would look).

Memory Retrieval

The two main types of retrieval are recall and recognition. Some memories can be context-dependent (can only retrieve memories if in the same environment when they were originally encoded) or state-dependent (can only retrieve if in the same mood as the memory was stored). In an exam situation, answering essay questions calls upon you to recall as much information as possible, whereas the multiple choice calls upon recognition of the correct answer.

Case Study of a Wrongful Conviction in Which Eyewitness Testimony Played a Significant Role: John Jerome White

September 21st 1979, while already under investigation by an agent of the Georgia Bureau of Investigation (GBI), John Jerome White was arrested for the rape, assault, burglary and robbery of a 74 year old woman who had been found asleep on her couch by the perpetrator during the break in. The incident occurred six weeks *prior* to White's arrest on 11th August 1979, and even though White maintained his innocence, he was convicted of the charges and sentenced to life in prison for the rape plus 40 years for the other charges on 30th May, 1980.

The evidence against White from the original crime scene included pubic hairs from a sheet that had been on the couch during the rape, and a piece of skin near the couch thought to be from someone's hand or foot. A composite sketch was developed using the victim's description, and a GBI agent that was investigating White on another charge considered the sketch similar enough that White was arrested. The GBI agent later testified that when White was arrested he had a cut on his hand – which could be related to the piece of skin found at the scene. From a photo line up, the victim was "almost positive" her attacker was White as she picked him out, then consequently picked him from a live line up later. All this evidence, along with a microscopic analyst testifying that the pubic hairs were considered "similar enough to say they have the same origin" saw White convicted.

White was released on parole as a labelled sex offender in 1990, a stigma that may have contributed to the drug possession and robbery convictions that saw him back in prison in 1997 to finish his life sentence. It was through the Georgia Innocence Project that saw a law student organise a DNA test of the preserved pubic hair from the original crime scene, that proved another man had committed the crime of which White had been convicted, and White walked free on the 10th December, 2007. Prosecutors then charged James Parham with the rape based on the DNA evidence, and he subsequently pleaded guilty and was sentenced to 20 years in prison (Innocence Project Website on John Jerome White).

Having the advantage of hindsight allows an extremely critical retro-perspective on the set of events and multiple factors that let up the arrest and conviction of John Jerome White. In order to examine these factors in closer detail, I have split them into two main categories: estimator variables and system variables.

Wells, Memon & Penrod (2006) describe estimator variables as variables that affect witness accuracy that are not under the control of the justice system. Eysenck (2009) and Wells et. al (2006) both suggest that issues such as the cross-race effect (or in-group expertise, where people are more accurate in recognising same-race faces), the weapon-focus effect (when individuals are likely to pay more attention to an attacker's weapon to the determent of recalling other potentially relevant information), and stress (where research has found that high levels of stress or anxiety reduces an eyewitness's ability to recall information and accuracy in identifications). Eysenck (2009) also suggests that eyewitnesses with face-blindness (Prosopagnosia) would be unreliable eyewitnesses, and that unconscious transference is a potentially dangerous variable, when an eyewitness misidentifies a familiar yet innocent face is misidentified as responsible for a crime. Wells et. al (2006) explores further to include several more estimator variables, including exposure duration (increased exposure to a suspect positively correlates with correct identifications), disguise (eyewitnesses are much less accurate at identifying a suspect who has changed their appearance), retention interval (as memory declines over time, any delays in identification can reduce accuracy) and witness intoxication (intoxicated eyewitnesses at the time of the crime lead to fewer correct identifications).

So, what estimator variables were present during the John Jerome White investigation and identification? It is fair to say that the victim was under a tremendous amount of stress during her ordeal, marking this item a definite estimator variable. It would seem from several recounts of the crime that the intruder did not attempt to mask his identity, however the victim did admit that the lighting in her apartment was poor and she was not wearing her prescription glasses (Innocence Project Website on John Jerome White) – thus allowing the estimator variable of disguise to become included as issue in the case. When the victim did pick White from a photo line up, she suggested she was "almost positive" that he was the attacker, which to me insinuates that she was not convinced that he was the attacker either.

System variables are issues that are within the control of the justice system after a crime has been committed. These can be broken down into two categories: utilizing an eyewitness's recall memory through interviewing, and calling upon an eyewitness's recognition memory through the identification of subjects (Wells et. al 2006 and Eysenck, 2009). Wells et. al (2006) and Eysenck (2009) suggest that some of the major dangers with interviewing an eyewitness include closed-ended questions (such as "what colour was the car" versus "what can you tell me about the car"), interrupting the eyewitness whilst in the middle of saying something, and following a pre-determined order of questions – no matter what the response is. Wells et. al (2006) also goes on to illustrate occasions when police interviewers either consciously or subconsciously led the witness to make inaccurate memories through leading questions; something Binet (1900) was able to demonstrate with his suggestibility experiments that revealed that incorrect information could be planted successfully. Out of these issues it is challenging to identify any one point that was present during the John Jerome White investigation, other than to say that the investigation took place in 1979 – 1980, and the cognitive interview (a researched interview technique that resolves many if not all of the interview issues listed above) was not developed until the early 1980's (Wells et. al, 2006). It would therefore be reasonable to infer that the victim could have been exposed to leading questions and other poor interview techniques at the time. Loftus (1992) argues that eyewitnesses are susceptible to accept misleading information presented after an event, then regard it as their own memory for that event later. Perhaps this influenced her identification?

This leads us onto the other category of system variables; the identification of suspects. Wells et. al (2006) lists the main areas when the justice system has control over the variables involved with the identification of subjects as composition sketches and line ups. The experiment of Koverea, Penrod, Pappas & Thill (1997) was carried out by former class mates of high school students, on 50 composite sketches. Results strongly suggested that composite sketches have a poor likeness of the original face as only 3 of the 167 names offered to match the faces were correct. Although another study has indicated that accuracy towards the original face can increase when multiple eyewitnesses independently produce composites (Bruce, Ness, Hancock, Newman & Rarity, 2002), it does not help those eyewitnesses or victims who find themselves left alone to identify the perpetrator – as was the case with John Jerome White. The victim was clearly alone with the real attacker – James Parham – in what she admitted was poor lighting without her glasses. From this she assisted in creating a "sketchy" composite that studies suggest faces the challenge of being dissimilar with the original face (Wells et. al, 2006). Other issue that arose from White's composite was the GBI agent thinking the sketch resembled White. There is every possibility that the agent was already biased towards White already as he simultaneously investigating him on another matter. If this is the case, there's every chance the agent influenced the victim during the line up selection.

Which brings us to discussing the system variables of line ups. There are four main ways these are done; target present and target absent line ups that are either photo or live line ups. One of the clear areas where bias and influencing of the eyewitness can occur is in the instructions leading up to the line up, with the most important point being whether the eyewitness is told that the suspect may or may not be in the line up (Wells et. al, 2006). The selection of the other members of the line up is equally important, where the description the eyewitness had previously given of the suspect should be taken in to account to ensure the suspect does not stand out obviously in the line up (for example, if the suspect is known to be Asian, it would be wise to have more than one Asian in a line up). In White's case, there were two line ups; the first was a photo line up where the victim (as mentioned above) was almost certain White was her attacker, then a live line up – where White was the only person to appear twice. This could have increased the risk of unconscious transference, when the victim then chooses White as he now looks familiar (Eysenck, 2009).

There are a number of procedures and safeguards that can be applied to reduce or completely remove some of these variables – more so the system variables than the estimator variables – as these are under more control. With the eyewitness interviewing there has been the development of the cognitive interview which is based on the encoding specificity principle and caters to the fact that memory is complex and information is accessed from several angles (Eysenck, 2009). There has also been the development of the PEACE Model of interviewing, which has become standard procedure in many countries within the police force (Davison, 2012). Improvement in identifying suspects can be achieved through: 1-to-1 sequential line ups, increased number of people in line ups, improvement on correct instructions before line ups, the proper selection of fillers so target doesn't stand out, double blind line ups where the officers with the eyewitness themselves don't know who the suspect is, and an improvement on composite software and knowledge that the more eyewitnesses that make sketches improves the likeness to the actual face (Wells et. al, 2006). To reduce estimator variables, the introduction of the expert witness in court explaining the fallibility of memory has shown to increase jury awareness and caution (Eysenck, 2009).

References

Binet, A. (1900). *La suggestibilité* [On suggestibility]. Paris: Schleicher.

Bruce, V., Ness, H., Hancock, P. J. B., Newman C. & Rarity, J. (2002). Four heads are better than one: Combining face composites yields improvements in face likeness. *Journal of Applied Psychology, 87*. 894-902.

Davison, J. (2012). *Interviewskills: Practical Guide to Investigative Interviewing.* Interviewskills Interview Training & Consulting. Auckland NZ.

Eysenck, M. W. (2009). Eyewitness Testimony. Chapter 14 in Baddeley, A., Eysenck, M. W. & Anderson, M. C. (Eds.). *Memory*, 317-342. New York N.Y.: Psychology Press.

Innocence Project – *The Innocence Project – Know the Cases: Browse Profiles: John Jerome White*. Retrieved March 29, from http://www.innocenceproject.org/Content/John_Jerome_White.php

Koverea, M. B., Penrod, S. D., Pappas, C. & Thill, D. L. (1997). Identification of computer-generated facial composites. *Journal of Applied Psychology, 82*. 235-246.

Loftus, E. F. (1992). When A Lie Becomes Memory's Truth: Memory Distortion After Exposure to Misinformation. *Current Directions in Psychological Science 1*. 121-123.

Wells, G. L., Memon, A. & Penrod, S. D. (2006). Eyewitness evidence: Improving its probative value. *Psychological Science in the Public Interest, 7*(2), 45-75.

Investigative Interviewing

Parents are investigators with their children. Peers are investigators with each other. Employers are investigators with employees. Recruiters are investigators with applicants. Consumers are investigators with salespeople, just as salespeople are investigators with consumers. Just because the subject of the investigation is not criminal in nature, does not make it any less important and any less of an investigation.

"An interview is a conversation with a purpose"
- Jonathan Davison

The Main Objective of an Investigator

The main objective of an investigator is to obtain information and evidence in search of the truth, and witnesses and victims are a major source of this information. As we noted in the Introduction to Memory section, memory is not perfect; memory can be extremely subjective with many areas when inaccurate information can appear genuine to the interviewee. This must be kept in mind when there is suspicion that a subject's story is not accurate. They may or may not be lying.

Seven Principles of Investigative Interviewing

Directly from Jonathan Davison's *Practical Guide to Investigative Interviewing*, these principles act as a great guide for an investigative interviewer (Davison, 2012).

1) The role of investigative interviewing is to obtain <u>accurate and reliable</u> information from suspects, witnesses or victims in order to discover the truth about matters under investigation.

2) Investigative interviewing should be approached with an open mind. Information obtained from the person who is being interviewed should always be tested against what the interviewing investigator already knows, or what can reasonably be established.

3) When questioning anyone, an investigator must act fairly in the circumstances of each individual case.

4) The interviewer is not bound to accept the first answer given. Persistent questioning is necessary sometimes.

5) Even when the right of silence is exercised by a suspect the investigator still has a right to ask questions.

6) When conducting an interview, investigators are free to ask questions in order to establish the truth; except for interviews to be used in criminal proceedings of child victims of sexual or violent abuse, as they are not constrained by the rules applied to lawyers in court.

7) Vulnerable people, whether victims, witnesses or suspects, must be treated with consideration at all times.

An Introduction to the PEACE Model of Interviewing

The PEACE framework is an extremely popular structure and method for investigative interviewing, which is made up of five stages. This information has been gratefully provided by Jonathan Davison (Davison, 2012):

Planning and Preparation
Engage and Explain
Account, Clarification and Challenge
Closure
Evaluation

Planning and Preparation: Consider these points during the planning and preparation phase of all interviews:
i)   How this interview might contribute to the investigation?
ii)   What is known about the interviewee and what needs to be established?
iii)   Legal requirements.
iv)   Offences and "Points to Prove".
v)   Practical Arrangements.
vi)   Pre-interview briefing of solicitor and management of active defence.
vii)   Prepared statements prior to interview.

Engage and Explain: This is the first phase of the actual interview, establishing a relationship between interviewer and interviewee. Engage is to encourage conversation, and explain is when the interviewer clearly explains the purpose of the interview so the interviewee understands. This includes:
a)   The reason for the interview (they may not know why)
b)   Routine that will be adopted (explain people, roles, use of recordings etc)
c)   Outline of the interview (to establishing the truth, do not edit anything out of account, as much detail as possible, no fabrications, their rights etc.)

Account, Clarification and Challenge: This phase is obtaining the fullest account that the interviewee (witness, suspect or victim) can or will provide. To obtain an accurate and reliable account the interviewer needs to:
- Obtain the interviewee's own uninterrupted account
- Expand and clarify their account
- When necessary, challenge the interviewee's account.

The Cognitive Interview fits into this category (more detail on the cognitive interview later). Keep track of what has been covered, and note any new information that has been introduced by the interviewee. Be aware of areas when the interviewee refuses to answer or says; "No comment", when there are areas that require challenging, and any inconsistencies with their own statement or other evidence.

Challenging an Interviewee's Statement:

1) The timing of your challenge: Allow the interviewee to finish telling their version of events first.
2) Adopt a clarification seeking approach: Explain that you wish to explore a particular point again, presented in a questioning manner rather than a confrontational one to avoid them going on the defence.
3) Ask for clarification of the discrepancies: Put these clearly and ask the interviewee for suggestions of how these differences have occurred.

The purpose is to be open in your search of the truth.

The role of the second interviewer is to watch the interviewee (micro expressions and body language), pay attention to the language used in responses and descriptions, and ask questions for clarity wherever needed, working in with the lead interviewer.

Closure: This phase summarises what has taken place, and ensures that the interviewee knows what will happen next. Provide contact details if anything further comes to mind.

Evaluation: This is evaluating the information obtained and how it may affect your initial interview planning and objectives, consider any re-evaluations (e.g. is the person still a suspect?), and evaluate your own performance (e.g. any areas where you need to improve?).

Research confirms that understanding a subject's culture and motivation then building rapport without revealing what your intent is the most effective interrogation technique.

An Introduction to the Cognitive Interview

The cognitive interview was initially developed by psychologists Geiselman and Fisher in the early 1980s due to the request from police and legal professionals to improve the practices of police interviews when gathering information from eyewitnesses. The standard police interview was characterised by constant interruptions, predetermined questions no matter what the answer, and poorly timed questioning.

The cognitive interview brings together the study of communication and cognition, therefore one of the primary aims of this process is the effective exchange of information between the witness and the interviewer through effective communication (Wells, Memon & Penrod, 2006).

According to Hess & Gladis (1987), good interrogation skills are similar to that of someone in advertising and marketing. The interrogator establishes credibility, feelings of reciprocity, gives compliments, conveys a sense of urgency and casts doubts on current beliefs – all the while building rapport.

Cognitive Interview Procedure

Step 1: Build rapport.
(i) Personalise the interview.
Exchange names. Make sure the witness is comfortable and is willing to try to remember as much as possible. Ask the witness to give as many details as possible but not to guess or fabricate.
(ii) Transfer control to the witness.
Tell the witness that you do not have knowledge of the event and it is the witness who holds all the relevant information. Let the witness choose the starting point for the narrative and give the account at his or her own speed and in his or her own words. Do not interrupt the witness, if at all possible. Listen actively to what he or she has to say. Allow for pauses.

Step 2: Recreate the context of the original event and ask the witness to report in detail.
To reinstate context, invite the witness to close his or her eyes and place him or herself back at the scene.

Step 3: Open-ended narration.
(i) Request narrative description.

Ask the witness to give a narrative account of the event in his or her own words. If clarification is required, use open-ended questions. Do not interrupt the narration to ask questions, although prompts such as "tell me more" may be used. Avoid judgmental comments and closed (yes / no) questions.

(ii) Focused retrieval.

This is not a technique but a general guideline to follow to help the witness concentrate on what he or she is describing by:

- using open-ended questions
- allowing for long pauses
- not interrupting the witness when he or she is speaking

(iii) Extensive retrieval.

Encourage the witness to search through his or her memory more extensively by asking him or her to report details from a number of different perspectives and in different chronological orders.

(iv) Witness-compatible questioning.

Time questions appropriately so they are compatible with the witness's retrieval pattern rather than adhering to a protocol.

Step 4: Closure.

Be sure to leave time to brief the witness and let him or her know what might happen next. Exchange contact information and encourage the witness to get in touch if he or she remembers additional details.

Other Comments on Memory and Interviewing

Each individual has a different frame of reference (upbringing, education, stereotypes, knowledge, attitudes, beliefs etc). These can alter how an interviewer questions a subject, and can lead to inaccurate information if the interviewer is bias in any way.

Assumption is the death of a good investigation.

Accurate memory recall requires the subject to speak without interrupted in the right scene. This may take some time and should not be rushed. Also – **confidence does *not* guarantee accuracy!**

If you suspect that someone is deceiving you, ask them to tell their story backwards. A guilty subject has a harder time remembering fictitious details in reverse.

CHAPTER 18
Various Applications of Reading Faces, Interpreting Body Language and Spotting Lies

"Understanding emotional experience applies not just to your relationship with others but to your relationship with yourself. It can help you understand the most private, personal, unique part of your self. This is a part of your self which has enormous power over your life" - Dr Paul Ekman

Introduction

This chapter is dedicated to telling the short stories of people who utilise reading faces, interpreting body language or detecting deception – or any combination of these – in the "real world". I originally had the idea of gathering stories of how successful body language professionals got into their fields, what was life like before becoming educated in non-verbal communication and how they use these skills both personally and professionally. However after reading the excellent book *Nonverbal Communication – Science and Applications* (Matsumoto, Frank & Hwang, 2012) I decided to also include some brief stories of people who are *not* body language professionals. Hopefully by now I have hammered my point home that it is useful for *anyone* to become proficient in this area; for becoming a more aware parent, effective salesperson, well-armed negotiator as well as a more astute consumer.

Adrian Solis – Federal Officer

A few years ago if you would have asked me to logically assess a person's emotional state based on non-verbal actions, I wouldn't have been able to intelligently describe anything of the sort. I became very interested in the subject and read many books but it wasn't till I found the SDL website and took the 101 training program that all the reading and information became clear. Because of the investment into this program, I'm able to proficiently determine a person's emotional state before interacting with them or as I watch them from a distance. This knowledge has enhanced my communication skills with co-workers and the public which is very important in my line of work. Being able to identify anger or a person suppressing anger is a useful skill to know in my work environment also. This understanding of non-verbal communication makes it possible for me to take appropriate actions to avert a hostile situation from taking place by addressing the issue with co-workers so they can approach these individuals with caution. So far my new found knowledge has made work much easier and I am no longer blinded by what was once unpredictable.

Anne-mari van Staden – Forensic Psycho Physiologist & Polygraph Examiner

As a forensic psycho physiologist, I work with people day in and day out and my customers depends on me to detect any type of deception.

I studied law but didn't quite fit in, nor did I find it interesting. I wanted to have an ever-changing challenging exiting career. It started with courses into body language followed by extensive training as a Polygraph Examiner. During my studies I discovered Forensic Interviewing and started specialising in it. This led to my micro expressions training.

When I introduced the polygraph to New Zealand in 2009 by opening the first polygraph company in the country, one of my first assignments was to do a polygraph on a prisoner that was sentenced for rape and attempted murder. By the time I met Mr. X he had already spent several years in prison. His father was very ill and Mr. X merely wanted to prove to his family before his father passed on that he was innocent. As the polygraph is only 98% accurate I decided to first do a forensic interview on Mr. X, followed by the polygraph examination. I needed to be 100% sure before making my conclusion as to his innocence.

Mr. X passed his forensic interview and polygraph. I went back to prison after a week and again did a polygraph on Mr. X. I was 100% sure that this inmate has been stuck in prison for a crime he didn't commit. Mr. X went on to be granted parole and has in the meantime obtained extra evidence relevant to his case. He has the support of his family back and a team of lawyers working on his case.

Micro expressions and body language make up the core of a forensic interview. Without it, it would only be an interview where no insight can be gained. My knowledge of micro expressions gave Mr. X back the support of his family and changed their lives.

Ben Maher – Behavioural Consultant & Retail

I have found since learning about non-verbal communication (through the SDL 101 and 202 courses) that my ability to interpret body language and facial expressions has improved immensely. My work in retail has benefited greatly as I now have much better communication skills and am able to see what people are really thinking, and move the conversation accordingly. It has helped me identify when a customer may be unimpressed with a product, or be thinking that it may not be suitable for them but not verbalising their hesitance. I can then proceed to address the issue, all without an actual spoken objection from the customer. This ability to "intercept" has resulted in a lot of positive feedback from customers, as they feel like they are having their own personal needs seen to, and not just given a generic sales pitch.

In retail you learn how to deal with objections, but these are always responses to *verbal statements*. Becoming proficient with non-verbal communication has helped me deal with objections before they are even verbalised (by interpreting micro-expressions and body language), which makes the whole process run much more smoothly for both parties.

I am also a pretty socially awkward kind of person. I sometimes find it difficult to make conversation or know what to do when a conversation stops. After learning about body language and verbal analysis, I am now much better equipped to interact in social situations. Being able to read between the lines and interpret social cues has not only added to my social skills, but has improved my overall confidence as well.

Of course the main thing I have gained from this is a greater ability to detect deception. After taking these courses and working with Stu I can now say I am quite good at detecting when someone is lying. I am often told I have a good eye for detail, I notice subtle things other people may not notice, but I never really knew how to interpret them. Learning about micro-expressions has revealed that I was picking up on something that didn't match up with what was being said – I knew something was off but I didn't know what. Once I became proficient with micro-expressions and matched this up with improved body language interpretation skills and a honed ability to analyse verbal style and statements, I find myself able to confidently identify when someone is attempting to deceive.

Blanca Cobb – Senior Instructor at Body Language Institute

The sight of the slightest twitch of fingers would send a chill down my spine. If a swift move to the belt on his waist followed that twitch, then my breath quickened and I'd tremble as I walked to my bedroom and assumed the position. My father would follow and the beating would begin. This incident repeated itself for several years during my childhood. At the time, I didn't realise that I was developing a keen intuition about body language. My safety depended on accurately reading my father's behaviours for his anger cues. I learned to tell the difference between regular anger and sinister anger by identifying his patterns of behaviours. I'd like to say that I was able to shield myself from the beatings; however, I couldn't. I plotted ways to distract him and delay the inevitable; however, my efforts were seldom effective.

I've trained with leading experts in the field, and I've flipped my childhood experiences into my life's passion of helping people understand body language and expose deception on both personal and professional levels. I offer private coaching, company training and keynote speaking. In addition, I'm a local and national media guest and have appeared on CNN, Good Morning America, CBS, FOX, ABC, NBC affiliates, where I highlight patterns of deceptive behaviours and point out the silent messages of body language in any hot media topic such as presidential and vice-presidential debates, child sex offenders and national murder cases. In other media interviews, I talk about and demonstrate how people can use body language to establish rapport and communicate more effectively within their families, careers and romantic relationships.

Bridget Dunn – Harcourts Real Estate

I've thoroughly enjoyed learning about micro expressions & body language! Becoming more aware of non-verbal communication has increased my ability to notice and accurately interpret the kids' subtle expressions and body language, as well as making a positive impact in my job. It's extremely helpful (particularly since I added the FACS Certification to my skills) to tell when a client is open to list their property – but even better is noticing if a buyer has reservations about a place, seeing it, then proactively asking questions to uncover and solve the problem.

Craig 'CJB' Baxter – International Bestselling Author of *Behind The Mask: What Michael Jackson's Body Language Told The World*.

Thinking back, life before non-verbal communication was both difficult and confusing. Like many others, I often used to think 'there is something I don't quite like about that person' and 'I don't think this person really likes me'. I wanted answers; I wanted to know why I felt like this about some people. It was only after learning about the fascinating world of non-verbal communication (otherwise known as body language) that I realised that important messages are being sent silently via a variety of bodily signals. I was always aware of something called 'body language'; however I, like many, thought that expressions and gestures were totally innocuous, a pseudoscience that served no importance in communicating. Oh how wrong was I.

I decided to investigate this fascinating topic 9 years ago. I focused most of my time on the teachings of Dr. Desmond Morris – A famous zoologist whose research into body language (especially *The Naked Man* and *People Watching*) revolutionised the study into how very much of our behaviour can be traced back to our primitive ancestors. Dr. Morris really opened my eyes into watching instead of listening. After reading a selection of Morris' work, it became abundantly clear that the thoughts I had previously (see above) could be traced back to the body language signals that someone was sending. Eureka! After discovering this literally life changing information, I set about educating the world about the importance of non-verbal communication.

Eric Goulard – Non-Verbal & Body Language Expert

In both relationships and professional life, communication plays a fundamental role between people. When two people meet, they don't know who is behind the image that the other sends. This image is often a mask that can hide many emotions. One partner intentionally shows a false smile by displaying the characteristics specific to the emotion they want to show. In doing so, they cheat on what others perceive them. Thus began the most basic lies. Everyone is a victim, every day! Husband, wife, business owner or manager. The smile is the first stop for false information as it can hide many emotions.

When you are trained in the recognition of emotions, you are able to receive signals that tell you a part of the story that is however not expressed by the other. Some of these signals are almost imperceptible, yet they bring you valuable information on what the other person is feeling. She might say something and feel the opposite – and as you are trained – you see it!

Your client may say: "I am being honest with you, you can trust me," and at the same time he shakes his head "no", a part of his body is tilted backwards and has already one foot in the direction of the door, ready to leave. This is not a good sign for you! He said something but his behaviour betrays his thoughts.

Mastering non-verbal communication is quite complex, and includes more than just gestures. Analysis should also cover the environment and the individual's interactions with it. How a person communicates using the objects surrounding them provides a lot of information about their stress level.

So, you have a real step ahead of your partner when you can decode behaviour and non-verbal communication.

Eyes for Lies (aka Renee) – Truth Wizard, one of only 50 people identified to have a naturally exceptional ability to spot deception.

Before knowing I had a unique ability to spot lies, read human behaviour and interpret body language, I felt like I lived in a world where I could understand people, but I was not understood. And this endlessly frustrated me. I would be in meetings with people, and I would identify to my confidants how someone was leaking anger or was inconsistent, and I could never understand why no one else saw what I did. It wasn't until I learned of my ability (Through the Truth Wizard Study) that I was able to put the pieces to together.

Facial expressions, words spoken, body language, emotions, attire, and demeanour all give us critical information about people, if we pay attention and it is the sum of the parts that often pinpoints inconsistencies. For example, if you meet a meticulously dressed man – hair perfectly in place, suit and shirt pressed to perfection, not a stray whisker on his face – this communicates a wealth of information to you; that the person before you is very concerned with appearance and is highly likely to be a neat freak or a person who likes to control their environment. If this person starts telling you that they are a sloppy person or that they lost something in a pile of their belongings, you have your first clue that something may be amiss. Their appearance reflects their behaviour, and here their words are contradicting a known behaviour. It's not a guarantee of a lie, but it is an immediate red flag!

On the contrary, if you meet a sloppy person who doesn't care about appearance, and isn't dressed to perfection and they try to tell you that appearance matters to them, you have a clue telling you the opposite – that they are either trying to fool you or they are fooling themselves!

Michael Lynes – CEO of Eutectics

I am not the overly-emotional type. I am more the "John Wayne-Bruce Wayne-Any-Other-Kinda Wayne" sort of person in my business, casual and daily interactions. I am not alone in this. To most of us men, emotions – subtle little imps – are generally not to be trusted and quickly lead to situations in which we feel simultaneously out of control and overwhelmed. Emotion therefore equals "Not Good" and is to be avoided at all costs.

This taboo attitude toward emotion is both stereotypical and fairly ubiquitous among males in the western world. We guys are just not encouraged to pay overt attention to emotion or display it in everyday situations.

Given the above, my current fascination with a discipline that is directly and intimately connected with the study of human emotion might seem both incongruous and somewhat gender traitorish. It goes by the catchy name of FACS (the Facial Action Coding System).

Mmmmm – OK – Facial Action Coding System…an intriguing, kinda-arcane, sorta-cool and most definitely (personal experience) eyebrow raising topic of conversation. Explaining FACS to your un-initiated relatives / friends is a fount of near-endless amusement – with two main reactions. You either one: get a wide-eyed slightly glazed insincere smile (the kind usually reserved for that sketchy guy you mistakenly got onto the elevator with, who starts opining loudly about his plan to overthrow the Federal Reserve System) or two: find yourself quickly filed under the 'harmless nut' category of party guests and are guided relentlessly to stand in a corner with the other numismatics, graphic novel (i.e. comic book) aficionados and baseball card collectors.

But FACS is not just a time consuming and useless hobby, nor it is the pseudo-philosophy of some weird little fringe group. It is, in my opinion, a very important and useful tool (hey guys – we *like* tools) that can with proper application and practice give you a highly effective advantage in dealing with emotion and emotional situations.

The main focus of this discipline, and by the way the reason I as an engineer find it so beautiful and fascinating, is the quantification (measurement) and analysis of facial expressions – and the identification of the underlying emotions that cause them.

Speaking for myself, my study and practice of FACS has literally opened up a new world of perception – or rather it has refined my ability to accurately perceive emotions – even when they are being actively suppressed or concealed. This new skill I find to be valuable and somewhat disconcerting; especially so when one applies FACS to the detection of intentional deceit.

Now of course there is a catch. FACS is not an easy thing to learn – it takes some concentration, dedication and several months of study and practice. There is a self-study guide available as well as courses taught by experts all over the world. And even after you complete the initial training and become certified, it takes lots of time and practice to become proficient. But I for one will vouch for the fact that if you take the time to acquire this skill – you will never again look at faces in quite the same way as you do now.

Robert Phipps – UK Body Language Expert and author of *'It's What You Don't Say That Matters'*.

Going back more than 30 years ago I knew nothing of the study of body language, what it was or what it could do for me. That was until I was caught out lying by someone who did know about body language as they were about to interview me for a job - great start for me!

They told me there and then they thought I was lying, and I was. I was intrigued as to how this sales director was able to instantly pick up that I was lying? I went through the interview and actually got the job, at which point I asked them outright.
"How did you know I was lying?" I asked.
"Your body language gave you away"

That was it, I'd just had my eyes opened to the world of Non-Verbal Intelligence, using his skills at reading body language cues and putting it to use for him in the business world. I decided to learn these new skills and apply them to my new career in sales and boy did it help. At one point I was the most profitable salesman in the company for two years running. Seeing as I was paid commission on the profit, it made sense to me to retain as much profit in a deal as possible and this is where reading the buyers body language was crucial.

Did I have to negotiate or could I see that the buyer was going to buy and was just trying to get the price down? I very rarely had to negotiate, I knew by the time it got to closing the sale whether or not the buyer was going to buy at the price I gave them - which most of them did - hence being the most profitable salesman.

Sachchidanand Swami – Certified Micro-expression Expert, Behaviour Analyst, and Accredited Researcher

Knowing and doing research about body language, kinesics, and non-verbal communication has changed my personal, social and professional life permanently. Especially the ability to read micro expressions (and gaining certification in area) brought more dramatic changes. Other than detecting lies, developing social rapport with people became much easier and faster. I've withstood many adversities successfully and also been able to capitalize on many opportunities.

By obtaining knowledge and proficiency in reading emotions and expressions, I could transform myself from the inside out much quicker. Today, this knowledge doesn't just help me only in writing good articles, but also in guiding and mentoring others (including doctoral Ph. D. candidates). Learning body language is not just about being able to read people and present ourselves more effectively, but also knowing how our ancestors would have succeeded in surviving.

Suzanne Masefield – Body Mind Analyst (AIBMA), Body Language & Micro-expressions Trainer

Did you know within 5 minutes of meeting, people decide whether they like, dislike, trust or mistrust each other? As a Body Mind Analyst (AIBMA), Body Language Specialist and Trainer, clients frequently ask what's holding them back, often not realising how they come across to others. They're unaware they shrink back, look nervous or alternatively come across as pushy, aggressive, deceptive or superior. Alongside being unaware of others subtle non-verbal messages, they miss vital cues to adapt their course effectively. This lack of awareness costs them dearly in personal relationships and professional aspirations.

Learning to read others via the subtle art of non-verbal communication, opens the door to a whole new world, allowing you to assess situations with greater accuracy, creating the difference between making or breaking relationships, getting a job or not, enhancing or sabotaging career prospects, increasing or losing wealth and heightening understanding and confidence when relating. In a study polling top executives in fifty-eight of the world's largest companies, every single executive named *'Communication Skills'* as a major factor in his or her advancement.

Employers make quick decisions about interviewee's perceived people / communication skills, determining whether they're likely to 'fit in'. When verbal communication mis-matches non-verbal behaviour, then instinctively we believe the body language gestures, over anything expressed e.g.: 'My last company was great', whilst exhibiting anger micro-expressions, tightened fists, shoulders pulled in, foot turned towards the door etc. Overcoming negative non-verbal behaviour increases positive results, whether it's finally daring to ask for a raise, deliver a great presentation, applying for a new job or admitting you're overworked and assertively standing up for yourself. Whilst in our evolving multi-cultural society, sensitivity to differing gestures between cultures is becoming more imperative to increase understanding, gain connection and avoid major faux pas that upset the status quo and break down communication.

Studies over the years suggest that between 55% - 80% of our communication is delivered via body language, so it makes good sense to learn this highly valued skill if you really want to get ahead in life.

Vicktorya Stone – Behavioural Consultant & Consciousness Consultant

The primary benefit in learning body language is that I can understand others more accurately and therefore connect with them in more authentic ways. With my coaching work, this is crucial. Especially with micro and subtle expressions, I can now see the flow of emotional reactions that are going on all the time, even when someone appears to be calm or neutral, or especially when they are trying to present a different face than what they really feel. **In this way I can help clients to draw out and recognise their feelings, even if they are unclear on their emotional state.** By pausing and asking a deeper question, and not resting with a casual response as the whole story, the core issue will be revealed much more quickly because I can now see what is obvious. There is always much more going on just below the surface. So in this area alone, knowing this art and science saves time in getting to the true feelings.

In more casual and social situations, knowing body language adds another dynamic layer of knowledge, so you can see quite a bit about what is going on between those you don't know. It may however spoil some fun in watching movies, as you'll notice more when actors aren't portraying genuine emotions or are unable to show certain feelings. There may even be a downside to learning body language for some. If others know what you do, especially by the term 'deception detection', they can become uncomfortable and feel like you're 'reading' them – even when you aren't. They may even avoid you! (But that would tell you something in and of itself!) I don't usually read others close to me in this way – as first of all the micro and subtle expression recognition requires some close attention and is a specialized skill taking effort – but mainly because it could take away from the welcome incongruity of social interaction. But when there is a serious moment, of course it is of utmost benefit to be able to get past any superficial response such as 'everything is fine', and realise whether the underlying energy is closer to anger or sadness, or some fear.

Being able to relate to others in more genuine and authentic ways is simply invaluable, and knowing more about body language – the language that is never silent – is priceless. I treasure the personalized training that I've had in this field with Stu Dunn, and continue to enjoy learning every day in this fascinating area of human behaviour.

Expert Testimony

I was being interviewed one morning by a local newspaper, and the subject of media cases came up – in particular, the reporter asked about New Zealand First MP Brendon Horan who (at the time) was under investigation for allegedly dipping into his late mother's bank account. In this instance, I hadn't seen any footage of Brendon Horan denying the allegations, so I couldn't comment, however I have analysed quite a few other cases. We briefly discussed Ewan Macdonald and David Bain, two New Zealander's who have been acquitted of murder, and the reporter then suggested I should be asked to review a number of live cases. Finally the reporter asked whether my reports would hold any weight in court.

This is a great question, one which has long bothered me. According to Arrigo & Shipley (2005) expert testimony is only used as evidence when the issue at hand is deemed to go beyond the experience of the jury members, and the expert "witness" is expected to hold a doctoral level in their field, be known as an expert amongst their peers, and have relevant training and experience. "The best expert witnesses are excellent teachers who prepare their information or message in a way that takes into consideration their audience" (Arrigo & Shipley, 2005), in other words, is able to explain things simply.

In the book *Outliers*, Malcolm Gladwell suggests the premise that to be an expert in your field requires a devotion to one's craft for at least 10,000 hours. Personally, I interpret the "10,000 Hour Rule" to apply to not just an expert in the field – but an elite. No matter the understanding, even someone with 20,000 hours under their belt in today's society may not be considered an expert in the legal system without a piece of paper saying so.

"An expert is a man who has made all the mistakes which can be made, in a narrow field." – Niels Bohr

Another issue with expert testimony in the behavioural sciences is the discrediting of the science by lawyers whose job is to ruin the testimonial. In my opinion, until behavioural sciences can be used in courts with the same weight as the polygraph, analysis and reports are extra pieces of evidence that can not and will not be used in court.

This is when it occurred to me while ranting on about how I believe behavioural sciences can actually be more accurate than the polygraph and how many people have been falsely sent to prison by so called "failed" tests alone – that we still have options. I would like to see in the future a meeting of non-verbal communication and behavioural sciences with authority and integrity. I would like to see behavioural science experts holding some weight in courts as expert witnesses. I would like to see the police consulting behavioural scientists more often – particularly with interviewing suspects and witnesses.

In 1896 a psychologist testified in court for the first time addressing inaccuracy in a witnesses memory during a murder trial.

And how will that happen? There are a few credible people out there doing analysis right now, with more than a few "home experts" born from fans of movies and television. For one thing, there's a danger that one group could hinder the future progress of the other.

1) I think that one responsibility the few credible consultants out there must do is to continue the work. Continue analysing and publicising opinions on the guilty or innocent, **backed by science**

not guesswork – as it could be *extremely* damaging to make a claim that someone is lying or is a murderer based on a few books that have been read.

2) Get the media involved. Smart media / reporters (newspapers, radio, TV, and of course the Internet) should make friends / follow / listen to the few credible consultants in their field. They can cover themselves by ensuring that any opinions are not shared by the media company, and will be able to skilfully negotiate around the hazards to avoid defamation.

I think the future of non-verbal communication and behavioural science in relation to expert testimony firmly sits on the shoulders of those who are already skilled in the science, application and careful interpretation – and to teach the next generation the dangers involved in jumping to conclusions, having preconceptions and making bold claims without thought of the implications.

CHAPTER 19
Relationships

"Failure to recognise each other's separate existence is the major source of conflict between partners"
- Harville Hendrix

Introduction

Throughout all of my studies of human behaviour, the subject that I discovered I was least proficient in was my own relationships. Somehow I managed to kid myself about my inability to understand the wants and needs of a significant other over the years, perhaps due to my background and that I generally pride myself on my communication skills?

Each relationship ended with my believing that I was right and their perspective was wrong. I truly believed that I knew better.

The shift in the way I saw relationships came in several ways. Meeting Bridget was one. We both made a commitment to learning how to better communicate with each other (as at the time we had perfected how *not* to communicate effectively). The next step in my journey was taking a road trip and listening to the entire *7 Habits of Highly Effective People* CD set (not for the first time) by the late Stephen Covey. And finally, the third shift in how I saw relationships came while reading Harville Hendrix's book, *Getting The Love You Want*. This combination created a complete shift in how I was looking at relationships, and I could see where I had gone wrong in the past prior to meeting Bridget.

I have placed this chapter at the end of the book, because I believe that in the end, everything is about relationships. It took me a long time to realise where I was going wrong, and once I finally experienced my paradigm shift, I felt the need to share at least some of what I learnt. It is my hope that people reading this chapter will gain renewed hope (where needed) for their own relationships, as well as providing some ideas of what to do to move forwards.

Relationships are like seasons in the sense that they go through stages that include romantic love, experiencing connection, fights and ruptures, repairs and make ups, then back to romantic love once more.

How Do We Pick Partners?

Something that I found most interesting was the cycle in relationships, when – once the person breaks up – claims that their ex-partner was just like the one before. Why is it that people are generally attracted to a certain type?

"We always marry someone for the purpose of finishing our childhood." - Harville Hendrix

According to Hendrix (2008) if you write down three positive and negative traits of your parents (or caregivers) on one page, and then do the same for your partner – you will discover several things (this is very simplified). First, your partner will likely share similar positive and negative traits to at least one of your parents. Secondly, the negative traits in each person should give you some reflection of some of your own negative traits that you do not like.

Relationship Observation #1: Most of your partner's criticisms of you have some basis in reality (Hendrix, 2008).

There is also a strong likelihood that the complaint is something from the person's childhood; for example the criticism from your partner that you are disorganised could stem from a parent or primary caregiver being disorganised and upsetting you as a child.

Romantic Love

Romantic love can be described as "a state in which a partner in a committed relationship assumes and lives as if his / her partner shares the same experiences and beliefs about the world." What actually happens is during the attraction phase of a relationship, is that the brain releases dopamine and norepinephrine (two of the body's many neurotransmitters) that help contribute to a "rosy outlook on life", a rapid pulse, increased energy and a sense of heightened perception. During this phase (when lovers want to be together every moment of the day) the brain increases its production of endorphins and enkephalins (natural narcotics) which in turn enhances a person's sense of security and comfort. There is also some evidence that there is an increase in the neurotransmitter serotonin (Hendrix, 2008).

"The meeting of two personalities is like the contact of two chemical substances: if there is any reaction, both are transformed." - C.G. Jung

Unfortunately the brain in not able to continuously pump dopamine and serotonin into our bloodstreams, therefore the "romantic love" phase is not designed to last. This stage of the relationship cycle is how people attract and bond with each other in order to be able to better deal with the rougher times.

Power Struggle

Hendrix (2008) suggests that the power struggle first occurs once a couple makes a real commitment to each other. Some time afterwards one or both partners begins to believe that the other has changed in some way (common comments are sayings such as; "You've changed" or "If you really loved me you'd know the answer"), which disrupts the connection made in romantic love.

"When we experience conflict, we experience fear, isolation and loss of awareness of connection, but not the fact of connection. Separation is an illusion." - Hendrix

Couples can feel disillusioned and frustrated with their partners during the power struggle, with a lot of relationships breaking up during this stage.

Relationship Observation #2: Many of your repetitious, emotional criticisms of your partner are disguised statements of your own unmet needs (Hendrix, 2008).

Have a think about this one, and ask yourself; "In what way are my common criticisms of my partner also true in me?" This follows the perspective that when you point a finger you have four pointing back at you – what can you learn about yourself in what you find most challenging in your partner?

"People are lonely because they build walls instead of bridges." - Joseph F. Newton Men

Choose a Conscious Relationship

Having an unconscious relationship infers that things happen without thought. That fight happened because they did this or that. They made me angry. Being in this space encourages blame and putting the other down or making them wrong. A conscious relationship however is taking ownership of your own behaviour, your own emotions, reactions and triggers. You become accountable for your actions, you intentionally work together, and ensure that each is heard and understood (as with body language, there is also a sender and receiver with verbal communication). You understand that each person has a valid perspective; and as their perception is different, take the time to investigate their point of view remembering that the key difference between sensation and perception is interpretation. Learn how to mirror each other. Validate what is being communicated by one another to ensure the intended message (from the sender) has been received as intended without incorrect interpretation (by the receiver). Learn how to empathise with each other.

Relationship Observation #3: Not being heard or feeling misunderstood is a great cause of conflict between partners (Hendrix, 2008).

I get frustrated when what I say isn't interpreted as I'd intended it, the wrong message is received. Every person is different, with unique experiences and perspectives. Therefore, when you come across this, ask your partner to tell you back what you just said. No Criticism. No judgment. Just ask; "Can you please paraphrase back to me what I just said, so I know you got what I meant?"

Closing Exits

Exits are what Hendrix (2008) refers to as behaviours that reduce or avoid involvement in your relationship. There are normal function exits such as work, and then there are intentional exits (also referred to as "the invisible divorce") that involves intentionally avoiding your partner. An example would be going to work (a normal functional exit), however knowing that things are not great at home and deciding to stay later at work, go out for drinks, start a new hobby or sport etc – these are all intentional exits. Other common intentional exits include reduced alone time with your partner, for some it may be television, others computer or games, perhaps the gym, or maybe reading. When things are not going well in a relationship, it is necessary to find the areas where you may be intentionally reducing or avoiding direct involvement in your relationship.

Identify them, and then work together to decide which exits can stay and which are unnecessary. Perhaps exercising is extremely important to you, therefore keep it. Maybe, however, watching three hours of television each night and going to bed when your partner is already asleep could change?

"Coming together is a beginning; keeping together is progress; working together is success." - Henry Ford

Relationship Myth: If you fight a lot with your partner you must be with the wrong person. Myth! Conflict is an opportunity to grow, and most "healthy" conflict allows this growth within relationships. It is when the conflict becomes damaging that something needs to change.

"Every word, facial expression, gesture, or action on the part of a parent gives the child some message about self-worth. It is sad that so many parents don't realize what messages they are sending" - Virginia Satir

Love Languages

Another book I found interesting was Gary Chapman's *The Five Love Languages* (Chapman, 2004). Again following along the sender and receiver perspective, Chapman (2004) suggests that there are five different ways in which people express love (quality time, words of affirmation, gifts, acts of service and physical touch), and the key to a healthy relationship is to understand not only how you receive love best yourself, but how your partner receives love. You buy your partner a gift when all they really want is quality time together. Learning how each of you receives love will help you to send more personalised "messages" to your partner. Find out your love language by visiting: http://www.5lovelanguages.com/profile/

Did You Know? The word "rapport" means "sympathetic relationship, have affinity with, harmony" (Concise English Dictionary).

"Some of the biggest challenges in relationships come from the fact that most people enter a relationship in order to get something: they're trying to find someone who's going to make them feel good. In reality, the only way a relationship will last is if you see your relationship as a place that you go to give, and not a place that you go to take."
- Anthony Robbins

THE LAST WORD

"A different suit will get you noticed for a day, but a change of attitude will get you noticed for a life time." - Lao Tsu

Thank You

I truly hope you have gained some insights from *True Lies; A Guide to Reading Faces, Interpreting Body Language and Detecting Deception in the Real World*. I have really enjoyed putting this book together, and wish you all the best in your continued learning in the fascinating world of the behavioural sciences. Please make sure you visit the SDL website, sign up for our newsletter, join us on Facebook and Twitter, and stay in touch.

What Now?

If you are reading the book through first with the intention of going back to the exercises, then resist the urge to turn the page to read the answers, but instead return to each section to complete. Remember back in Chapter 1: *How To Get The Most From This Book*, "To know and not to do is not yet to know"!

Continue to learn. There are some fantastic mentors out there – some of whom contributed to Chapter 18 of this book.

If you wish to continue or refine your learning with me, you have several options. The SDL 101 Certification: Introduction to Micro Expressions, Body Language and Detecting Deception has been extremely popular, and has my team and I working directly with you for 8 online modules. Each module has an assignment to do, and includes video analysis feedback – as of course it is very difficult to gain feedback on your learning by yourself.

For more information, visit www.microexpressions.co.nz/services.php

Contact us through the website www.microexpressions.co.nz/contact.php if you are interested in SDL running a 101 and 202 Certification Workshop in your area, or whether you would like customised training or consulting for your company.

You can visit the Emotional Intelligence Academy website www.emotionintell.co.uk for information on official Paul Ekman workshops. Although I am not associated with these programs, I believe they them to be some of the best in the world.

I wish you all the best with your education in non-verbal communication!

Warmest regards,

Stu Dunn
Founder of SDL Behavioural Science Consultancy

APPENDIX
Suggested Answers

"Better than a thousand days of diligent study is one day with a great teacher." - Japanese proverb

Part 1 Exercises – What Are These Expressions Saying

Image 1: Ashley Hebert

This expression appears after she hears the words, "Never apologise for that". Straight after this expression, she chews the inside of her mouth. In context, I believe she is demonstrating a teeth-clenched fear-like lip stretch (AU20) that gives the impression of guilt. The "ekk" sound goes well with this expression, and has an overall sad quality.

I would suggest fear with sadness.

Image 2: Mallory Hytes Hagan

Taken just as she was announced as the winner of Miss America 2013, this expression shows shocked surprise, which can also get easily mistaken with fear.

Image 3: Angelia Jolie

This image indicates a mixture of emotions – in particular: anger and distress. If you picked any forms of anger *and* sadness then you have done well on this image.

Image 4: Chloe Kardashin

As Chapter 8 mentions, this is a classic disgust-smile which does not look the least bit genuine to me. If you only noted happiness, that is still good. However, take a closer look at her smile – the eyes are not engaged and her upper lip is raised.

Image 5: Kate Middleton

This expression is what I would call polite amusement. The FACS codes for Kate are: 12C+13B+23A+25D+26C+52C+62D

Looking at the codes we can note there is no AU6 (necessary for genuine happiness). AU12 and 13 are two different kinds of lip raisers.

Image 6: Hugh Laurie

The FACS codes for Hugh's expressions are: 1C+4C+5C+L12B+R12A+52B+61B

On the codes alone, this could look like a nervous distress covered with a slight smile. Sadness is seen in AU1 (inner eyebrow raise) and AU4 (lowering of the brow) – with the 5 (raising of the upper eyelid) adding a slight fear aspect. The uneven smile (AU12) could indicate mild contempt or a masking smile to cover other felt emotions.

I believe that anyone suggesting sadness, fear or contempt is on the right track. In saying this, the expression could also be posed for the camera – this is the danger of making assessments from still images – we lack the context. This could also be indicating disbelief.

Part 2 Exercises – What Are These Images Saying?

Image 7: Victoria and David Beckham

Victoria: Her facial expression is a strange wide eyed blank look, very challenging to put an actual expression to it other than distant, disbelief, or even stunned. She is being led by David, her body facing a slightly different direction.

David: His expression looks angry, body turned, his arm back giving the impression of walking faster than Victoria. Perhaps the people taking the picture were annoying them?

Image 8: Renata Sorrah

Her expression looks like a form of sadness, with her hands across her chest and leaning forwards slightly hinting towards her saying something heart-felt.

This is the body language and expression I would expect to see on someone who has been falsely accused of something.

Image 9: Barack and Michelle Obama

Barack: Slightly raised eyebrows are all we can really tell about his expression. His body his turned with one foot pointing towards the door, his hand also pointing in the same direction. To me this indicates that he may be saying that he has a meeting, has to leave, etc.

Michelle: Tight lips and partial smile indicate to me she is feeling angry with an attempt to mask this with a smile. Her hands are in the broken zipper position, and her feet are in the cross leg position. Taking all of these signs into account, it would appear that she is not feeling very assured or happy.

Image 10: Prince Albert and Princess Charlene

Prince Albert: A small social smile on his face, sitting in a crotch display – however he is covering with a form of broken zipper and hold. It could be that Prince Albert is aware of Princess Charlene's unhappy mood and trying not to show it.

Princess Charlene: Her face looks distant, sad, with her arms folded in front of her. She looks to be making herself smaller.

Part 3 Exercises – Speech and Deception

<u>Voice Exercises</u>

"<u>Where was I</u>? *<u>um</u>* I was going for a walk then,"
E.g. Where was I? could be repetition, and *um* a speech error.

1) "I…think…it looks great,"
- Pauses.

2) "I d-don't *um* …know *cough*, …maybe, maybe one of the other kids took it?"
- Speech error (stutter), speech dis-fluency (um), pause, speech error (repetition). The cough could be a pause, speech error or dis-fluency.

3) "…I-I went to the store about 10 *um*, yeah, about 10,"
- Pause, speech error (stutter), speech dis-fluency.

4) "What year did I graduate? I graduated in 2005,"
- Could be a partial repeat, or a clarification. Overall, nothing wrong with this statement.

5) "Tell you a time when I…well…*um*…I – when I was there *um*. What did you want to know exactly?"
-   Pauses, speech dis-fluency, speech errors. Also, includes repeated statement.

6) "What time? Think it was 8 – no – 9 o'clock,"
- Nothing wrong with this statement, the quick correct usually indicates honesty.

7) "I have…never…we don't hit our *clear throat* kids. They're good kids,"
- Pauses, speech dis-fluency. Also, change of pronouns (I to we), and possible euphemism with using the word "hit".

<u>Verbal Style Exercises</u>

"Where was I Friday? I <u>do not</u> remember, <u>I am not</u> someone that keeps track of time,"
E.g. <u>do not</u> and <u>I am not</u> are non contracted denials

1) "We need laws that protect everyone. Men and women, straights and gays, regardless of sexual perversion…ah, persuasion…"
- Slip of the tongue.

2) *Question:* "Are we negotiating with any other media company?"
Answer: "We have not been negotiating with Mayfair Media,"
- Specific denial.

3) "I was not able to identify the perpetrator before they knocked me out and took Gail. Gail meant everything, please find them,"
- Non contracted denial. Also, formal language with the term perpetrator (which changes from one to "them"). Also, how did he know "they" took Gail when he was knocked out?

4) "It happened around 1 o'clock? I wasn't even home by then, I got home about 2:30,"
- Nothing wrong with this.

5) "People who do these sorts of things... you just don't do that sort of thing,"
- Pause and pronoun inaccuracy (the use of "you" don't just..).

Putting the Voice, Verbal Style & Statements Together Exercises

Label the following combining everything you have learnt so far in this chapter, from the voice, verbal style and verbal statements.

1) "Where was I Thursday night at 7 o'clock? I... I don't recall..., I- as I don't wear a watch it's hard to say. I t-think I was *clears throat*, yes, I was driving home,"
- Repeat (or partial) statement, pause and speech error (stutter), pause, more stuttering, speech dis-fluency. Not wearing a watch could be an excuse, and it was strange how the person decided they were driving home when they had trouble at the beginning of the sentence.

2) "I do not know what you are talking about; I do not frequent those kinds of places,"
- Non-contracted denials, and potentially a distancing statement (those kinds of places).

3) "To be honest, I love what you have done with the place. And frankly, I do not know what the critics were talking about,"
- Reinforcing statements, non-contracted denial.

4) "Did I punch him? *cough* No, I did not push him. I'm someone that keeps his cool,"
- Partial repeat, speech dis-fluency, euphemism (punch to push), protest statement.

5) "I got up, made breakfast, had a shower, then headed off to work about 7:30. The traffic was bad, so got to work about 8:45. When I got home the place had been trashed, including my stamp collection, which was insured separately,"
- Pronoun issues, too much / too little statements.

6) "I have people who do that sort of thing for me, why would I need to go there?"
- Distancing statement, potentially a protest statement.

7) "Fight? Yes, we had a disagreement that night, *um* b-but you've got to understand... that woman is difficult sometimes. It was not my fault – I mean that she left upset that night. My wife has done it before, so I was not worried,"
- Euphemism (fight to disagreement), speech dis-fluency, speech error (stutter), pause, distancing statement (that woman), speech error, possible euphemism (left upset), distancing (my wife), non-contracted denial.

8) "How dare you! You're the last person who can point fingers! Don't you remember the last time *you* made a mistake – you have no right accusing me of anything like this – have I ever done this before?"
- Guilt statements.

References

Association for Psychological Science, *The Psychological Study of Smiling*. Retrieved December 1, 2011, from http://www.psychologicalscience.org/index.php/publications/observer/the-psychological-study-of-smiling.html

Balomenos, T., Raouzaiou, A., Ioannou, S., Drosopoulos, A., Karpouzis, K., and Kollias, S. (2005). *Emotion Analysis in Man-Machine Interaction Systems*. MLMI 2004, LNCS 3361, pp. 318 – 328, 2005.

Chapman, G. (2004). *The Five Love Languages – How to Express Heartfelt Commitment to Your Mate*. Northfield Publishing, Chicago, IL 60610.

Darwin, C. (1913). *The Expression of the Emotions in Man and Animals*. New York: D. Appleton and Company p. 272.

Dictoryary.com, *Lying*. Retrieved November 21, 2011, from http://dictionary.reference.com/browse/lying

Duffin, S. (2009). *Reason in the Real World*. Dunmore Publishing Ltd, Wellington, PO Box 25080, New Zealand.

Eisenberg, Abne M., Smith, R. Jr. (1971). *Nonverbal Communication*, New York: The Bobbs-Merrill Company, Inc.

Ekman, P. (2009). *Telling Lies – Clues to Deceit in the Marketplace, Politics, and Marriage*. W.W. Norton & Company, Inc., New York, NY 10110.

Ekman, P. (2003). *Unmasking the Face – A Guide to Recognizing Emotions from Facial Expressions*. Malor Books, Cambridge, MA 02238-1069.

Ekman, P., & Friesen, W. V. (1974). Detecting deception from the body or face. *Journal of Personality and Social Psychology*, *29*(3), 288-298.

Ekman, P., Friesen, W. V., & Hager, J. C. (2002). *Facial Action Coding System*. Research Nexus division of Network Information Research Corporation, Salt Lake City UT 84107.

Fast, J. (1970). *Body Language,* New York: J.B. Lippincott, Inc.

Frank, M. G. & Svetieva, E. (2012). Deception. *Nonverbal Communication: science and applications.* 121-144, SAGE Publications, Inc, California 91320.

Frank, M. G., & Ekman, P. (1997). The ability to detect deceit generalizes across different types of high-stake lies. *Journal of Personality and Social Psychology*, 72, 1429-1439.

Frank, M. G., Feeley, T. H., Servoss, T. N., & Paolantonio, N. (2004). Detecting deception by jury, I: Judgemental accuracy. *Journal of Group Decision and Negotiation*, 13, 45-59.

Frank, M. G., O' Sullivan, M. & Menasco, M. A. (2009). Human behavior and deception detection. In J. G. Voeller (Ed.), *Handbook of Science and Technology for Homeland Security.* New York: John Wiley and Sons.

Goldstein, E. B. (2011). *Cognitive Psychology: Connecting Mind, Research, and Everyday Experience.* (3rd ed.). Belmont, CA: Wadsworth, Cengage Learning.

Hargrave, J. L. (1994). *Let Me See Your Body Talk,* Iowa: Kendall/Hunt, Inc.

Hendrix, H. (2008). *Getting The Love You Want – A Guide for Couples.* St. Martin's Press, 175 Fifth Avenue, N.Y. 10010.

Henley, R. P. (1977). *Body politics: Power, sex, and nonverbal communication.* Englewood Cliffs, NJ: Prentice-Hall.

Knapp, M. L. (1972). *Nonverbal communications in human interaction.* New York: Holt, Rinehart and Winston.

Matsumoto, D. (2011). Evaluating Truthfulness and Detecting Deception. *FBI Law Enforcement Bulletin*, June 2011, US Department of Justice.

Matsumoto, D. (2012). *Nonverbal Communication: science and applications.* 121-144, SAGE Publications, Inc, California 91320.

Meyer, P. (2010). *Liespotting – Proven Techniques to Detect Deception.* St. Martin's Press, New York, NY. 10010.

Nierenberg, G. I., Calero, H. (1971). *How to Read a Person Like a Book,* New York: Simon and Schuster, Inc.

Ophir, E., Nass, C., & Wagner, A. D. (2009). Cognitive control in media multitaskers. *Proceedings from the National Academy of Sciences*. 106, 15583-15587

Paul, P. (2009). *Kid Stuff*. New York Times.

Pease, A., Pease, B. (2009). *The Definitive Book of Body Language – How to read others' thoughts by their gestures*. Pease International Pty Ltd, PO Box 1260, Buderim, 4556, Queensland, Australia.

Porter, S. & ten Brinke, L. (2010). The truth about lies: What works in detecting high-stakes deception? *Legal and Criminological Psychology*. 15, p. 57-75.

ReadingBookOnline, *Mark Twain's story: My First Lie, and how I got out of It*. Retrieved November 21, 2011, from http://www.readbookonline.net/readOnLine/1005/

Rosenthal, R., & Jacobson, L. (1968) *Pygmalion in the Classroom*, New York: Holt, Rinehart, and Winston, Inc.

Vrij, A (2010). *Detecting Lies and Deceit – Pitfalls and Opportunities* (2nd ed.). John Wiley & Sons Ltd, West Sussex PO19 8SQ England.

Weiten, W. (2010). *Psychology: Themes and Variations*. (8th ed.). Belmont, CA: Wadsworth, Cengage Learning.

Wikipedia, *Facial Action Coding System*. Retrieved July 19, 2011, from http://en.wikipedia.org/wiki/Facial_Action_Coding_System

Wikipedia, *Body Language*. Retrieved December 1, 2011, from http://en.wikipedia.org/wiki/Body_language

Stu currently lives on the Kapiti Coast with his wife Bridget, teaches Wing Chun Kung Fu, is New Zealand's leading expert on micro expressions, body language and detecting deception, and implements these skills on a daily basis dealing with buyers and sellers in his successful real estate business .

www.MicroExpressions.co.nz
www.TeamDunn.Harcourts.co.nz

Caught in a lie

Shearer's face tells a sorry story of dodgy doings

True or false? Seven expressions recognised the world over

Learning body lang

Code to finding out who is lying

Is Dunne telling the *Truth*?

The face of 'Mr Sensible' tells a different story ...

Body POLITICS

Learning to read body language

Micro expressions a revelation

■ Ann Reading

INSCRUTABLE: Stu Dunn's cat is unworried by his micro expression owner's ability to read emotions.

Recog fictio

Made in the USA
Middletown, DE
25 January 2017